CROW

'Sax's book roams divertingly over the scientific and cultural history of the "corvid" family, which includes the carrion crow, the raven, the rook and the jackdaw, tracing ambivalent responses to the mischievous birds.'
– *The Guardian*

'A fascinating and delightful book . . . examines the crow in myth, literature and life . . . With sections on the crow in ancient civilisations, different parts of the world and through to modern times, this book would be an excellent read for anyone interested in this group of birds.'
– British Trust for Ornithology

'In this vivid and enjoyable meditation on crows in art, literature and history, Sax gives the genus *Corvus* the enthusiastic treatment it deserves.'
– *Publishers Weekly*

'This authoritative and well-researched volume is an ideal source for anyone who has been intrigued, annoyed or charmed by these wonderful birds'
– *Cage and Aviary Birds*

'*Crow* is the sort of monograph I treasure and seek out, a work that draws together around a "totem animal" centuries of relevant lore, a richness of iconographic treatments (photographs, portraits, masks, natural history plates, cartoons, book plates, marginalia, etc.) and the best natural history and natural science available to a lay researcher and engaged author.'
– *h-nilas Reviews*

'I found the section on the history of the scarecrow especially moving. Sax skillfully conveys the shifting use of these objects, which were first developed to serve a real purpose, scaring corvid crop predators, and slowly devolved into something less applied and more nostalgic. For me, this section, especially, captured the ambiguous relationship between humans and crows that is repeated throughout the book . . .'
– *Anthrozoös*

Crow

Boria Sax

reaktion books

Published by Reaktion Books Ltd
Unit 32, Waterside
44–48 Wharf Road
London N1 7UX, UK
www.reaktionbooks.co.uk

First published 2003
Reprinted with corrections 2007, 2010, 2012, 2015
This edition first published 2017

Printed and bound in Great Britain by Bell & Bain, Glasgow

A catalogue record for this book is available from the British Library

ISBN 978 1 78023 842 5

Contents

Preface to the
New Edition

ABOUT A DECADE and a half ago, the editor Jonathan
Burt asked me to write the first instalment in Reaktion
Books' new series entitled Animal, saying that I could
select any creature that I wanted. My choice was the crow, an
animal so multi-dimensional that there could be no question of
reducing it to any stereotype. My approach to writing *Crow* was
to cast aside many academic protocols, and simply concentrate
on all of the things that were special about my subject. At times,
I may have been almost as idiosyncratic as the corvids themselves.
The book has an ambiance and rhythm that could be difficult or
impossible for me to recapture today.

Parts of *Crow*, inevitably, are out of date. This applies especially to the discussion of the ravens at the Tower of London,
which I myself have shown to have been on the grounds only
since about 1883, and not, as the tourist guides claim, since the
reign of Charles II or earlier. The ravens were brought in as props
when the Tower of London was marketed to tourists as a Gothic
castle, with all the accompanying tales of ghosts, tyrants and
maidens in distress. Then, during the Second World War, the
ravens, with their keen senses, were used unofficially to give early
warnings of approaching enemy bombs and planes, an activity
which gave rise to the supposedly 'ancient' legend that Britain
will fall if the ravens leave the Tower. They have gone from

being avatars of doom to national pets, protectors of the realm and, perhaps most significantly, symbols of our precarious environmental heritage.

As to the more scientific parts of the book, that sort of material now dates almost as quickly as new software. Nearly every month seems to brings new discoveries that document the intelligence of crows. A team of scientists led by John Marzluff has shown that crows can recognize human faces, remember them for years, know what people have befriended or antagonized them and even pass on that knowledge to their offspring.

All of that confirms the thesis of *Crow*, which is that crows are perhaps the only animals that have not only a pragmatic but an intellectual interest in human beings. For no very apparent practical reason, they constantly observe us, and they are very good at interpreting human body language. Chimpanzees find it extremely difficult or impossible to learn what humans mean by pointing a finger, but dogs and crows understand this without being taught.

Many animals have relationships with humankind that, though determined by custom and utility, are as specific as any biological niche. These creatures include, for example, the dog, sheep, cat, deer and bee. In every case, the traditional relationships embrace rights, duties and mutual expectations. But the human relationship with crows is unique in its symmetry and reciprocity.

Both human beings and crows have the nuclear family as the basic unit of society, but also enter into larger associations. We may study crows, but they seem to study us even more. Crows do not mingle in our society but remain a tribe apart. Nevertheless, no other animal, not even dogs or cats, probably understands human beings as well. They can be our partners in dialogue, and, to the extent that we understand crows, we may learn a lot about ourselves.

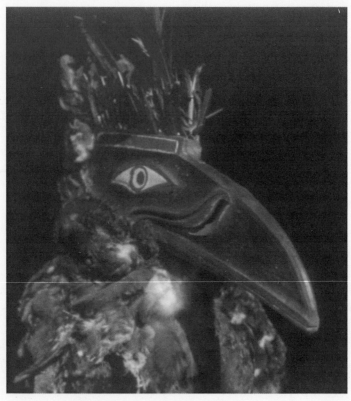

Shaman wearing a Kwakuitl raven mask, *c.* 1914.

Introduction

Corvie is a gay chap for all his inky coat.

SEAN O'CASEY, *The Green Crow*

T HOUGH COMMON in our cities and our country-
sides, crows rarely cast even a stray glance in the
direction of human beings. Their calls are not for us,
only for other crows. One day, however, as I was going home
in White Plains, New York, I saw a small, scruffy crow hopping
across the sidewalk in front of me. When I tried to take
another look at it, the crow seemed neither curious nor frightened. But, contrary to the usual habit of crows, it sometimes
appeared to meet my gaze. At first I thought the crow might
be hurt, and thought of calling the humane society or a vet-
erinarian. The crow, however, showed no sign of pain and
seemed to be rather less worried than I.

There were only a few square yards of grass alongside a busy
street, but it was enough to hold several trees, including one tall
pine. Looking straight up through the branches, I could make
out a nest near the very top. The crow was a fledgling, cast from
the nest so that it would learn to fly. Hardly anybody on that busy
sidewalk would pass without at least a glance in the direction of
the crow. Sometimes dogs or children would chase the bird, and
older people tried to talk to it or feed it. Neither greatly pleased

Two carrion crows in a French lithograph of 1907. Artists often render the special gracefulness of crows, although few viewers appreciate it.

nor troubled, the crow would politely hop away, and this continued for several days. The jumps turned into flights, and these gradually became longer. After about a week, I passed one day to see the crow was no longer there.

Actually, it is probably not very far away, but it prefers to keep a moderate distance from human beings. I can no longer tell that crow from others, which might be its children or parents, in the park, but I like to imagine that perhaps that crow may sometimes be discreetly watching me. Rejoining other crows after a brief sojourn in the world of human beings, it may carry happy memories and share these with other crows.

On the surface, relations between crows and human beings usually seem courteous but distant. Yet the importance of these birds in folklore shows that crows have an intense, if subtle, fascination for men and women. When one looks at other birds in an urban setting, such as pigeons or sparrows, they generally seem to be simply biding their time, relaxing and picking up bits of food. With crows, by contrast, there always seems to be something important going on, some domestic drama that is being acted out. They fly energetically about and call to one another in unpredictable ways.

And what is a crow? No image of an animal is simpler, more iconic and more unmistakable. We think of a silhouette of outstretched wings, a slouched head and an extended tail against the white of a winter sky. Such, at least, is the poetic view, but the way scientists see things is a lot more complicated. They tell us that crows are members of the family Corvidae, which also contains magpies, jays, choughs, nutcrackers and other birds.

These birds belong to the order Passeriformes, popularly known as 'songbirds', even though not all the members are musical. The family Corvidae probably originated in Australia, at a time when that continent was relatively isolated from Eurasia. After the continents drifted closer together, about 20 to 30 million years ago, these birds crossed into Asia. That migration was followed by a period of rapid evolutionary differentiation, as the birds spread to Europe and America. Members of the family Corvidae are now found everywhere in the world except for the southern tip of South America and a few relatively small areas near the poles.

The word 'crow' is occasionally used broadly for all members of this avian family. It is often used more restrictively for members of the genus *Corvus*, also known as 'true crows', which includes ravens, rooks and jackdaws. Finally, the term may be used, perhaps a bit unscientifically, for those members of the genus *Corvus* that do not have any other common name.

In this book we will look at the relationship between human beings and crows from many perspectives – including those of poetry, taxonomy, animal behaviour, myth, legend and the visual arts. If it occasionally seems hard to believe that the poets and scientists are talking about the same thing, we can think of the famous story from the Hindu *Udana* known as 'The Blind Men and the Elephant'. Seven blind men were presented by a rajah with an elephant and asked to describe it. One felt the head and said that the elephant was like a basket, while another felt the tusk and thought the creature resembled a ploughshare. The one who touched the trunk thought of a plough, while the one who embraced the body said it was a granary. Still others, who touched different parts, claimed the creature was a like a pillar, a mortar, a pestle or a bush. The tale is generally told to illustrate how different creeds, though apparently opposed to one another, may all be parts of a single truth.

Of course, we are not talking about creeds here but about cultural perspectives. The 'blind men' here are illustrious poets, scientists, priests, painters . . . and they are not examining an elephant; they are examining a crow. Nevertheless, the same principle applies. All of the various forms of cultural activity are, after all, ultimately part of a single tradition, and together they can yield a far more comprehensive picture than any one alone. In this book I will move back and forth between science, poetry, legend and other traditions in recounting the history of crows and human beings.

These birds are mostly black, though some species have areas of white, brown, grey, blue, purple or green. This dark plumage generally makes crows stand out dramatically, though it can also

The arms of the house of Corbet, showing the raven in an endearingly human aspect.

Raven illustrated in a 19th-century book of natural history. The raven is by far the largest and most imposing of corvids.

make it difficult to distinguish individual birds. Black is the colour of earth and of the night, hence crows have often been associated with mysterious powers. It is a colour that can make creatures appear more imposing and more serious, which is why it has been preferred for the robes of priests and, until recent times, of schoolmasters.

Their slouching posture, and their love of carrion, have helped to make crows symbols of death, yet few if any other birds are so lively and playful. They indulge in such apparently useless games as carrying a twig aloft, dropping the toy, then swooping down and catching it. For no apparent reason, they may hang upside down by one foot or execute back flips in flight. Crows in Alaska reportedly break pieces of congealed snow off sloping rooftops and use these as sleds to slide down. Lawrence Kilham, who

Blue jay, after J. J. Audubon, from a 19th-century book of natural history.
This is one of the most familiar corvids of North America, and its
playfulness has often made it a trickster in legends.

later wrote an important work on the social behaviour of corvids, once took a shot at a raven in Iceland. A single feather dropped to the ground and the raven flew off. As Kilham stopped to reload his gun, the raven returned and flew over his head. The purplish remains of the cranberries the raven had been eating fell on his hat, and Kilham concluded that ravens, in addition to being smart, had a sense of humour.

Foraging on their long, powerful legs, crows can appear to glide over the earth. Then they ascend almost effortlessly, flapping their wings only now and then, into the air like spirits. Though people generally do not think of them in such terms, crows are also remarkably graceful. From the tip of a crow's beak to the end of its tail is a single curve, which changes rhythmically as the crow turns its head or bends toward the ground. The best known members of the genus *Corvus* are the carrion crow (*Corvus corone corone*), the hooded crow (*Corvus corone cornix*), the American crow (*Corvus brachyrhynchos*), the common raven (*Corvus corax*), the rook (*Corvus frugilegus*) and the jackdaw (*Corvus monedula*). All these birds have extensive ranges, and complex relationships with human beings.

The carrion crow is almost entirely black, though its feathers show a purple or green gloss in certain lights. The hooded crow has a large area of pale grey on the back of the neck and lower breast. Otherwise, the two subspecies are almost identical, and they interbreed freely where their ranges overlap. They have probably only diverged since two populations were separated during the last ice age, and their combined range covers most of Eurasia. The hooded crow is generally found in the far North, the Mediterranean, Eastern Europe and Central Asia, while the carrion crow is common in Western Europe, Korea and Japan.

Eurasian nutcracker from a 19th-century book of natural history. Though not a true crow, the nutcracker shares the reputation for intelligence of its close relatives. It has an uncanny ability to cache food and locate it at a later date.

Jay from a 19th-century book of natural history. This bird is known for its ability to mimic the voices of other animals, from crickets to humans.

The American crow is similar to the carrion crow in size, about 40 centimetres or 17 inches at maturity, and colour, and some researchers believe the two should be considered a single species. The reason they are not is mostly a matter of geography. To belong to a single species, animals must habitually interbreed, but the carrion crow and the American crow are separated by oceans. The American crow is found in a wide range of habitats throughout the United States and Canada but not outside of North America.

The common raven is, despite its name, not often sighted, but it has an enormous range. It lives throughout most of the northern hemisphere and north of the Sahara in Africa. It is substantially larger than other crows, with a length of about 65 centimetres or 27 inches at maturity. It also has a heavy beak and an especially deep voice. When flying directly overhead, the common raven can be distinguished from most other crows by its wedge-shaped tail and comparatively pointed wings. It is also notable for alternately flapping its wings and gliding.

Still another corvid to be frequently confused with the carrion crow and the raven is the rook. We can distinguish the rook primarily by the rough, pale area around its eyes and beak. This can make the faces of rooks appear wizened and very expressive. These birds are most common in Northern Europe, but their natural range extends eastward as far as Japan. They were introduced in New Zealand, a region previously without corvids, during the nineteenth century.

The one member of the genus *Corvus* that nobody will confuse with the others in appearance is the jackdaw, which, at a length of only about 25 centimetres or 10 inches, is far smaller than the rest. It has a short, pointed bill and is grey about the

THE MAGPIE.

'The Magpie' from a 1911 British *Natural History*. Although not considered 'true crows', magpies share crows' reputation for intelligence.

shoulders and upper breast. The most dramatic feature of jack-daws, however, is their silvery eyes, which shine dramatically against the dark feathers surrounding them. Jackdaws are found throughout Europe and in the western part of Asia. Their habit of chattering as they flutter about has given them a special reputation for mischief.

There are over twenty to thirty additional members of the genus *Corvus*, depending on just which classifications are pre-ferred. The brown-backed raven (*Corvus ruficallus*) is found through most of the southern hemisphere, including Australia, Africa and parts of Latin America. The Indian house crow (*Corvus splendens*) and the jungle crow (*Corvus macrorhynchus*) are found throughout much of southern Asia. Several members of the genus *Corvus* are confined to relatively restricted habitats or even particular islands.

Today, the taxonomy of crows, like that of other animals, is the subject of arcane debate among specialists. The distinctions between species of corvids may often be both useful and elegant, but they will seldom or never help us in understanding references to crows in legend or literature. In folklore it is hardly ever possible to know for sure which corvid is meant in a passage. Prior to the eighteenth or nineteenth centuries, varieties of birds and other creatures were distinguished only loosely, usually by features such as colour. The blackbird was sometimes confused with the carrion crow, even though the two are not closely related, simply because they had similar plumage. But to enter into the spirit of archaic tales, we must be able to lay aside some of the knowledge that we have acquired. When writing about mythology, one cannot always use the language of science.

Crows are found less in the grandly systematized mytholo-gies of Europe and Asia than in the earthier realm of legend.

A jackdaw and an American crow, from a 19th-century book of natural history. The artist has depicted the jackdaw as a thief, while the crow has an almost heraldic dignity.

The majestic cosmologies of official creeds feature animals that are fanciful or exotic – dragons, unicorns or lions. But legends, which may have survived for millennia in oral traditions, can often be older than myths. Formalized mythologies are generally products of warrior and priestly classes. Folklore generally expresses a more egalitarian, and perhaps more archaic, vision of the world, in which not only kings and peasants but animals and plants interact with comparative intimacy. This is the genre in which crows, which are used to living off their wits, fit in especially well.

Even the names of corvids are often primeval. Other animals are mostly named according to their associations in mythology or daily life. The various words that designate corvids generally derive from attempts to imitate their calls. One example is our word 'crow', which comes from the Anglo-Saxon *cráwe*. It is related to the German synonym *Krähe*, which is even closer to the cry of the bird. Another example is the word 'raven', which comes from the Old Norse *hrafn*. Etymologists trace that word further back to the prehistoric Germanic *khraben*, a pretty good transliteration of the raven's call. It is related to the Latin *corvus*, the Old Irish *crú*, the Sanskrit *karavas* and near synonyms in several other Indo-European languages. The name 'jackdaw' is based on the combination of 'daw', an old Anglo-Saxon word for 'fool', and 'tchak' or 'Jack', the call of the bird. The word 'rook' comes from the Anglo-Saxon *hróc* or, in a more modern form, 'croak'. The name 'magpie' is, according to one theory, a combination of 'Margaret' and 'pied', suggesting a brightly dressed lady. The Latin name of the bird, however, is *Pica pica*, which is probably an evocation of its voice. The designations seem magical, since to name the bird is, in a sense, to summon it with a call.

There is an ongoing dispute among scientists as to whether the American crow, the raven, or any of their various relatives is the

The arms of the Barons von Rindscheit, symbolizing perhaps the union of the strength of the boar and the wisdom of the crow.

most intelligent. All ornithologists agree, at any rate, that corvids are at or near the pinnacle of the avian world in brains, perhaps rivalled only by parrots. Corvids have the largest brains in relation to their body size of any birds, and corvid brains are tightly packed with neurons. The brain of an American crow is about 2.3 per cent of its body mass. For human beings, the brain is about 1.5 per cent of the body mass, while the figure for a domestic chicken is 0.1 per cent. For the common raven, it is about 1.3 per cent, though those birds have, at 12–17 grams, the heaviest brains of any birds in absolute terms.

'Intelligence' is a concept with a mythic resonance in contemporary society. Everybody agrees that it is terribly important, but nobody knows what it is. Scientists generally agree that a precise definition of 'intelligence', transcending lines of species, is probably impossible. Popular thinking, however, is not always so modest or cautious. Intelligence is often enough used as a measure not only of certain abilities but of the entire worth of a person or animal. We traditionally think of intelligence as the quality that sets human being apart from beast and, perhaps, animal apart from plant.

Their intelligence, together with the whiskers around their beaks and an apparent smile, makes crows, in a scruffy sort of way, endearingly 'human'. Nature writer David Quamen has written that 'the entire clan' of corvids 'is so full of prodigious and quirky behaviour that it cries out for interpretation not by an ornithologist but a psychiatrist'. His theory is that the natural intelligence of crows is far in excess of what is demanded for survival in their biological niche. The result is that they are continually bored and make up games to amuse themselves. In other words, crows are like very bright children in environments where intellectual accomplishments are neither encouraged nor appreciated.[1]

A fable traditionally attributed to the Greek sage Aesop, said to have lived on the isle of Samos in the sixth century BC, told how a thirsty crow found a pitcher full of water. On finding that the pitcher was too heavy to knock over, the crow started pitching pebbles into the top until the water level had risen and it could drink. The first-century encyclopaedist Pliny the Elder reported that people had actually seen a raven during a time of drought piling up stones in a memorial urn that contained rain. Through most of the twentieth century, scientists believed birds utterly incapable of such reasoning. In the 1970s, however, American scientists observed a captive blue jay (*Cyanocitta cristata*), a bird closely related to crows, pick up a stick and use it to sweep stray bits of food within pecking range of its cage.

Plenty of observers, including highly sophisticated scientists, have reported remarkable mental feats by corvids. Some researchers believe that a variety of crow found on the island of New Caledonia in the Pacific is, after humankind, the most proficient toolmaker among animals. Its 'toolbox' includes a poker made of a pointed twig, with which it pokes for grubs among the fronds of palm trees. There is also a hook, carefully sculpted from a curved twig, with which to draw grubs out from hollows. Perhaps most remarkable of all, there is a saw made from the skeleton of a leaf, which it uses to slice and impale grubs. All these tools are constructed with remarkable care and deliberation.

Carrion crows in the city of Sendai in Japan have discovered an ingenious way of cracking walnuts. They take the nuts and wait beside the road until the light turns red. Then they descend, place the nuts in front of the wheel of a car, and fly off. When the light turns green, they return and eat the pieces of nuts that a vehicle has crushed. When fishermen in Finland leave their lines in holes that have been cut in the ice, hooded crows systematically draw out the twine from the water and steal the catch. Many researchers over the past several decades have also reported incidents that confirm the intelligence of crows. One crow in a laboratory figured out how to scoop water from a plastic cup and carry it away to moisten pellets for food. Another used a piece of paper to push scraps of food within pecking distance of his cage.

Probably the most dramatic proof of corvid intelligence came in 2002 from the Oxford laboratory of scientist Alex Kacelnik. He took two New Caledonian crows (*Corvus moneduloides*) named Abel and Betty, and confronted them with a puzzle which turned out to be far too elementary for such clever birds. They were supplied with buckets of food in a tube and given

A Northern raven and Canada jay by Louis Agassiz Puertes, 1936. The thick feathers enable these two corvids to thrive in frigid northern latitudes.

two wires, one hooked and one straight, to pull these out. Immediately recognizing which was the appropriate tool, Abel made off with the hooked wire. Betty then carefully bent the remaining wire, made a hook, and retrieved her meal. Presented with the task several times, she not only solved it repeatedly but improvised new ways of bending the wire. Sometimes she held it down with her feet and bent it with her beak; sometimes she wedged one end with sticky tape and twisted the other. Chimpanzees and monkeys were presented with the same task, and none could grasp how to accomplish it. In White Plains I have noticed how crows have figured out where and when restaurants will take out their garbage. They wait by the dumping ground and then systematically tear open plastic bags to get at the food. Just about everybody seems to have a 'crow story', an observation of corvids that reveals their unusual intelligence or their emotional awareness. Anecdotal accounts may be suspect, particularly from the point of view of a scientist. Inevitably, these incidents involve not only a record but an interpretation of behaviour, and accounts by even a careful observer are easily influenced by subjective feelings or by assumptions of human superiority. But even if we remain a little sceptical of individual accounts, the sheer number of tales about crows shows how the birds have a way of surprising people.

Researchers consider linguistic facility an important indication of intelligence. According to one study, 23 distinct calls of American crows, things such as calls to assembly or warnings of danger, have been deciphered. This is a vocabulary that the great apes might envy. There are dozens of other calls made by crows and ravens that seem meaningful but have yet to be interpreted. Some of these calls are particular only to a specific region or even to a single pair. Each crow has a special call by which it is recognized by its companions. Furthermore, crows are remarkable mimics. They copy the calls of owls and probably other animals in the wild, and crows in captivity have been taught to use fragments of human language. Much of the communication between crows is probably made through combinations of sounds and gestures. Such interaction may be subtle and precise, yet, like intimate communication between human beings, so dependent on context that outsiders to the community – including people – will never be able to decipher it.

This verbal facility is also reflected in folklore. The raven and the carrion crow say relatively little to human beings in legend, yet their occasional words are heavy with significance. An English pamphlet of 1694 told that a raven in Herefordshire three times said, 'Look into Colossians, the third and fifteenth.'² But it is the magpies and jays that are most renowned as chatterboxes. This has often given them reputations as tricksters in cultures from North America to China. Their verbal facility has also earned them reputations as lovers, demons and fairies.

Another sign of intelligence is a complex social life, and that of corvids continues to challenge researchers today. Crows often hunt and scavenge cooperatively. A favourite trick is to find an otter that has just caught a fish. One crow will nip at the otter's tail, making it drop the catch and turn, and then another crow will immediately pick up the fish.

The basic unit of crow society is the extended family, which centres around at least one breeding pair. American crows, for example, need about three years to reach maturity and breed. A couple may have a brood every year. Those crows that have not yet reached breeding age or have failed to find a mate will stay with their parents and help to raise the next brood, assisting especially in the building of nests. A comparatively long lifespan,

Illustration of a blue jay from Eaton's *Birds of New York* (1910). Its bright colours and loud call help make this bird one of the most noticeable in North America.

sometimes more than two decades, enables crows to develop familial ties over generations. Crows have courtship dances, in which they lower their wings and make their tails quiver, and their sexual relationships are monogamous. Ancient Egyptians thought of crows as models of domestic harmony.

Many crows, including the carrion crow and the American crow, form large assemblies in late autumn or winter. Sometimes they number in the thousands (occasionally over a million), but the reason remains something of a mystery. It might, for example, be primarily for protection from predators, or to exchange information about foraging areas, or to find mates. It could also be some combination of these and other reasons. According to legend, the meetings were for the purpose of 'holding court'.

The most solitary crows are ravens, who generally live as couples or small families in remote, often mountainous areas, though even they occasionally congregate to form groups of hundreds and even thousands. The comparative isolation of ravens, together with their imposing size, makes them especially potent symbols of destiny. The most social crows are rooks and jackdaws, which form colonies, with a great many nests in a single tree or an abandoned building.

Corvids and people even share a special intimacy with the canid family. Scientists in North America have observed a symbiotic relationship between wolves and crows or ravens. Ravens

'The Rook' (*Corvus frugilegus*), an illustration by Jann Sepp of *c.* 1790. The rough, bare skin of this bird's face can make it appear somewhat like a fierce, helmeted warrior.

follow wolf packs, and then eat the remains of animals the wolves have killed. Corvids also call the attention of wolves to carcasses, and then eat some of the meat after the wolves have torn open the skin. Ravens in North America, and probably elsewhere as well, even play a sort of game of 'tag' with wolves. They dive at wolves, provoking the lupines to chase them; at times ravens, in turn, chase the wolves. Packs of wolves and flocks of ravens sometimes produce a sort of 'concert' together, in which the howling of wolves alternates with the cries of ravens. The bird and mammal share both a common grandeur and an association with destruction, and they are linked in many mythologies. Both, for example, would accompany the Norse Odin, god of magic and of battles.

One may debate whether it is a sign of intelligence or of foolishness, but another quality that corvids have in common with humans is a love of shiny objects. Smaller corvids, such as magpies and jackdaws, are especially notorious for stealing jewellery. In their collection of German legends, the Grimm brothers tell how,

Hooded crow from a 19th-century book of natural history. Farmers are often ready to forgive crows for eating their grain, so appealing are these birds.

in the seventeenth century, a corrupt official used a jackdaw to steal the entire treasury from the city of Schweidnitz, one gold piece at a time. Such suspiciously 'human' behaviour could even arouse fears that the birds were the familiars of witches.

The similarities between crow and human can often lead to enmity as well as to affection. Like humans, crows are omnivorous, though they have a special fondness for carrion. One tale from Somalia told how the birds held an assembly to decide how the food in the world would be divided up. The clever raven proposed that all birds larger than he should eat flesh, while smaller birds should eat plants. The proposition was accepted, but what the others did not realize is that it left the raven free to eat anything.

But before the twentieth century, when human society across the globe was overwhelmingly rural, crows would constantly have been seen pecking at the bodies of dead animals. Most significantly, they would be seen tearing the entrails of dead, and even dying, soldiers on the battlefield. They even learned to follow armies in anticipation of a meal. But the idea of being eaten by crows could at times be comforting, especially in cultures that prefer to view life as a continuous cycle of birth and decay. Corpses were traditionally fed to birds in parts of Persia and India. In Tibet the custom of feeding the bodies of the deceased to scavengers, particularly crows and other birds, lasted until the 1950s. To make the dead easier for birds to eat, the mountain people would cut the corpses into small pieces. The bones would be ground and kneaded with barley in order that they would not be left scattered on the ground.

The eating of carrion has caused crows to be closely associated with death in cultures throughout the world. We should remember, however, that attitudes towards death have always been

Satiric illustration by J. J. Grandville from *Les Animaux* (1866), showing the staff of a hospital. The shark, a master surgeon, gives instruction to ravens, rats and vultures.

complex and ambivalent. It brings at once terror and comfort. It can be viewed as extinction, or as the passing to another, perhaps more blessed, realm. All of this ambivalence extends also to crows. Legends throughout much of the world make them instructors for the living and guides for the deceased.

The Murinbata, an aboriginal tribe of Australia, tell that Crab and Crow once argued about how it was best to die. To demonstrate her way, Crab found a hole, cast off her old shell, and waited patiently. Finally, Crab returned with a new shell, and announced she had been reborn. Crow objected that the process took too long. Then he fell over backwards, lay motionless, and could not be revived. Human beings may have remained subject to mortality, but Crow had at least shown a quick and dignified way to pass on to the next world.

The lore of crows is rich and varied, yet a few themes come up over and over again. In a vast range of cultures from the Chinese to the Plains Indians, crows are bearers of prophecy. A good example of that is the practice sometimes known as 'counting crows', used with both magpies and crows to predict the future. The counting is often done when corvids are seen flying overhead. Folklorists have recorded many rhymes, especially in Britain and America, linking the number of crows you see with fate. The counting is often done when corvids are seen flying overhead. One of the best-known verses for counting crows is from Scotland:

> One for sorrow, two for mirth,
> three for a wedding, four for a birth,
> five for silver, six for gold,
> seven for a secret, not to be told;
> eight for Heaven,
> nine for Hell,
> and ten for the Devil's own sel' [self].[3]

The symbolism of the numbers varies greatly from one version of the rhyme to another.

Today, every corner of the globe has been explored, and cameras are even sent to Mars and beyond, yet at least since the early

Another satiric illustration by J. J. Grandville from *Les Animaux* (1866), showing an old crow writing down her travel experiences.

nineteenth century, Romantic poets such as Blake and Keats have complained of disenchantment in the world. Our longing for wonder can no longer be satisfied by journeys to exotic lands or even, for the most part, by exploring the obscure corners of the human psyche. The symbol of transcendence is no longer the phoenix or the unicorn, though these images retain their beauty. Whether we live among cornfields or skyscrapers, a far more resonant symbol is the crow. Crows are among the most ubiquitous of birds, yet, without being in the least exotic, they manage to remain mysterious.

one
Mesopotamia

Think of the ravens. They do not sow or reap; they have no
storehouses and no barns; yet God feeds them.

LUKE 12:24

THE BIBLE ITSELF is not read or quoted nearly as
often as it was a few generations ago. Nevertheless, the
images and cadences of the Judaeo-Christian scriptures
still echo powerfully in our culture. Every creature that even
appears in the Bible retains a heightened significance. The raven
or crow is mentioned ten times in the Old Testament and once in
the New. There are far more biblical references to the sheep, the
central animal of the Hebrew economy, and the dove, an archaic
symbol of divine love. But no other creature appears in such varied
contexts, or with such symbolic ambiguity, as the crow or raven.

In the human imagination, crows have always been creatures
of extremes. They are playful and solemn, noisy and articulate,
sacred and profane. Many crows are completely black, but legends throughout the world tell us that they were once white. The
Near East has always been a setting for great dramas of good and
evil, ecstasy and misfortune, and, as might be expected, crows
have often had an important role.

The Bible has but a single Hebrew word, *orev*, for many varieties of crow. It may be derived from *erev*, meaning 'evening',

because the dark colour of the birds is like the darkness at the end of day. Poetry, if not necessarily scholarship, marks the many biblical references to such birds as ravens, with their austere and terrifying beauty. That is how the references have been translated from ancient times until today.

Ravens especially, though habitually shy of humans, thrive in rugged terrain such as that of the Near East. When crows and ravens emerged from their nests in the mountains, it would often be to feed on the slain. Though the sight of ravens might bode ill for villagers, their toughness often won them admiration as well. Most crows are highly social, but the solitary raven is at home in rocky valleys and hills.

Stories of ravens in the Near East go back far before the sacred texts of Judaism and Christianity. In the fragmentary Babylonian epic of king Naram-Sin, from the library of the Assyrian king Ashurbanipal, men with the heads of ravens invaded from the

In this illustration from a 19th-century popular scientific book, the raven is given an anthropomorphic scowl, suggesting his fierceness. In the background a raven looks on without pity while waiting for a ram to die.

Prominently placed near the centre of this Assyrian relief is a bird, possibly a raven, that has arrived to feed on the bodies of those slain in battle.

mountains of the north. The king at first thought that they might be demons, but then found that they would bleed like human beings. Perhaps the invaders may have been warriors wearing helmets with nose guards that protruded like the beaks of ravens.

In the Sumero-Babylonian epic of Gilgamesh, a sole man, Ut-napishtim – antecedent of the biblical Noah – tells of how he and his wife survived a flood that destroyed the remainder of humanity by building a boat. The waters had finally begun to recede, and the boat came to rest on the mountain of Nimuh. To send out birds to see in which direction they would fly was a common practice among mariners in the ancient world, used to determine the proximity of land. After seven days, Ut-napishtim sent out a dove, but it found no resting place and returned to the deck. He then sent out a swallow, but it soon flew back as well. Finally, he sent out a raven, which ate, preened itself, and did not turn back. Then Ut-napishtim knew his ordeal was at an end and made a sacrifice in gratitude to the divinities.

Much the same story is told of Noah (Genesis 8:6–12) as of Ut-napishtim, though with a few important variations. The Ark of Noah had come to rest on Mount Ararat. First, Noah sent out a raven, but it circled back and forth and did not bring back news of land. Then Noah sent out a dove, which found nowhere to perch and returned to the Ark. After waiting for seven days, Noah again sent out a dove, which returned with an olive branch in its beak.

As the story of Ut-napishtim evolved into that of Noah, a second dove was substituted for the original swallow. More importantly, the failure of the raven to return took on a meaning that is the opposite of the original. Instead of signalling the presence of land, which is actually the most reasonable interpretation of the raven not coming back, it became a dereliction of duty.

Jewish, and much of Christian, tradition holds that animals did not eat meat until after the Flood, since they would otherwise not have been able to live together in the ark. The raven, as a bird of prey, is considered an unclean beast according to Jewish law, as laid out in Leviticus and elsewhere. One commentary on the story of Noah in the Talmud holds that the raven was not sent out to find land but expelled from the Ark for a crime, perhaps for attacking some other creature or for copulating in the Ark. Others tell that the raven did not return because it began pecking at the floating bodies of the dead. In the Talmud the raven sometimes engaged in spirited arguments with Noah. At one point in the *Sanhedrin*, the raven complains that seven of every clean species have been preserved but only two of his, then suggests that perhaps Noah has sexual designs on his mate.

If we think of the Ark as a grand experiment in the domestication of animals, perhaps the story of Noah and the raven records the inability of certain animals to follow human direction. Folklorists have suggested that the story may at one point have been an etiological tale, where the raven had originally been white but was cursed for failure to return and turned black. At any rate, neither that nor any other punishment, if such it be, of the raven is recorded in the Bible. The story of Noah and the Ark has become – for Jews, Christians and Muslims – a decisive turning point in the relations between humanity and nature. According to many traditions, it is only with the New Covenant of Yahweh (that is, God), after the Flood had subsided, that people lost the ability to understand the speech of animals. But crows and related animals, especially magpies, have cadences that resemble those of the human voice. One widespread legend in Europe is that the magpie was not allowed in the Ark because it made too much noise. Instead, it stood on the roof, chattering constantly as cities sank beneath the waves. A British legend tells that the magpie is a cross between the first dove and the raven sent out by Noah, which is why it is both black and white.

In subsequent biblical passages, ravens appear to be agents of God. When hiding from King Ahab, whom he had condemned for erecting an altar to Baal, the prophet Elijah took refuge in the wilderness. Yahweh ordered ravens to bring the prophet bread in the morning and meat in the evening (1 Kings 17:6). But how, and exactly what, did the ravens feed the prophet? Some secular commentators have suggested that Elijah may have used the raven to lead him to dead animals. But in that case, or even if the ravens simply brought him carrion, there are some very serious problems from the point of view of Jewish tradition. As mentioned previously, ravens and their relatives were explicitly numbered among the 'unclean' birds in the Bible (Leviticus 11:15). Furthermore, carrion was so detestable to the Hebrews that whoever so much as touches a carcass will be unclean until evening (Leviticus 11:24). Food from ravens, if it were anything like what the birds normally eat, would not have been kosher.

Jewish commentators sometimes have resolved the problem by saying that the ravens brought Elijah food from the table of King Jehosophat. But how did they know which of the king's dishes were kosher?

One biblical passage has even suggested to many people that God has a special love for ravens: 'Who makes provision for the raven when his squabs cry out to God and crane their necks in hunger?' (Job 38:41). The *Yalkut Shimoni*, a commentary on the Talmud compiled in the thirteenth century, explains this love by telling how a raven taught Adam and Eve to perform the first burial. After their son Abel had died, the first man and woman did not know what to do. A raven killed a companion, dug a hole in the ground and buried the body, and the human couple buried their son in imitation. Out of gratitude for their help to Adam and Eve, God feeds baby ravens until their black feathers have grown, at which point their parents take over.

At times in the Bible, the raven is used as a symbol of desolation. The book of Zephaniah states that after the destruction of Edom, 'the owl and the raven will live there' (2:14). The book of Isaiah states that after the ruin of Assyria, 'the raven will croak at the doorstep' (34:11). Ravens or crows have also been scourges of God:

> The eye which looks jeeringly on a father, and scornfully on an ageing mother,
> shall be pecked out by the ravens of the valley.
> (Proverbs 30:17)

But the Bible also accords ravens a special magnificence. In the Song of Songs, the hair of the bridegroom is praised as being 'black as the raven' (5:11). Much like human beings, ravens seem to be constantly renegotiating their relationship with God.

German illustration of Proverbs 30:17 from the mid-18th century. In the foreground a young man mocks his parents. In the background we see the fate that awaits him – that of having his eyes plucked out by ravens after his death.

two

Egypt, Greece and Rome

Everything has gone to the ravens!
THEOGNIS (sixth century BC)

THE REPRESENTATIONS of corvids in the cultures of the ancient Mediterranean reflect the developing attitudes towards the natural world. The Egyptians, who did not make a sharp division between the realms of nature and humanity, thought of crows with robust affection and good humour. The Greeks continued that tradition, yet they also sometimes looked to corvids with fear, awe and nervous laughter.

The Greeks viewed nature as having vast and inexorable powers, which might be feared or placated but seldom controlled. They were perpetually engaged in wars, in which the vanquished might expect to be either slaughtered or sold into slavery; there was also repeated devastation from famine or plague. Corvids were often seen pecking at the dead bodies of animals or even people, and they were not often welcome in a world where life was extremely precarious. For the Greeks, corvids represented the realm of nature persisting even in cities, creatures largely beyond the control of either human beings or gods.

The vast Roman Empire of Augustus and his successors over the next few centuries did, for all its internal conflicts, bring a certain security to its citizens. While wars continued, they were usually on distant frontiers. People might think of themselves, if not necessarily as 'masters' of fate, at least not as helpless victims. The Greek tragedians and lyric poets would regularly lament the human condition, but the Romans generally accepted it with neither celebration nor complaint. While the Greeks constantly emphasized the fragility of human accomplishments, the Romans believed their empire might last until the end of time. The Roman view of nature was less fearful and more bucolic, increasingly so as the population of Rome increased to over a million and huge plantations worked by slaves replaced smaller farms. The Romans could view ravens and crows with an affection that would have been almost unthinkable in Greece.

Crows in Egyptian art often appear feeding on crops, less frequently on bodies scattered on a battlefield. They appear beastly, usually in an endearing sort of way, and almost 'human', but – unlike, say, the ibis or the falcon – not divine at all. The Turin satirical papyrus from the Ramesside period (1307–1070 BC) includes a picture of a crow ascending a ladder into a sycamore-fig tree with wings outstretched, as a hippopotamus gathers a basket of figs from its branches. The Egyptians kept various meticulous records of business transactions, but they wrote down very little of their mythology, and we know the stories of their divinities primarily through accounts by Greeks and Romans. Aelian, a Hellenized Roman of the second century AD, reported that the Egyptian pharaoh Moeris used a tame crow to carry messages to any destination he might name.

According to Horapollo, a Graeco-Egyptian priest from the third century BC, the crow was important in the symbolism, if not necessarily the religion, of Egypt. Crows represented faithful love, for, as people of the ancient world correctly observed, they are

Zeus, his priestesses and two crows – the 'black doves' of Dodona –
appear in this anachronistic illustration of a Greek myth
painted in the Middle Ages.

monogamous. Horapollo wrote that when the Egyptians wished
to show the union between Aries, god of war, and Aphrodite,
goddess of love, they would draw two crows. This was because a
crow would always lay two eggs, from which a male and female
would usually be hatched, and the two offspring would live
together for their entire lives. When, Horapollo explained, occasionally two males or two females would hatch together, they
would be doomed to a life of celibacy. For that reason, the sight
of a single crow was a bad omen, but a pair of crows symbolized

marriage. Young crows symbolized restlessness and irascibility, since a mother crow fed her young on the wing.

Doves share the reputation of corvids, though with less justification, for monogamy. There is, however, much difference in the symbolic emphasis of the two kinds of birds. Doves are associated with idealized, and often divine, love, while corvids represent marriage in all its earthy reality. While doves are used to symbolize courtship, crows represent its consummation. Horapollo also wrote that the symbol of a widow who would remain faithful to her husband was a black dove, since these birds mate for life. Since black doves do not normally occur in nature, it is likely that Horapollo was referring to a corvid here as well. The Greek historian Herodotus also mentioned black doves in a famous passage written during the fifth century BC.

Herodotus wrote that two black doves flew up from Thebes in Egypt, one to Libya and the other to an oak tree in the grove of Zeus at Dodona. The dove in Libya directed the people to make an oracle to the god Ammon. The dove in Dodona spoke in a human tongue, telling the people that the grove would be a place of divination. By the time of Homer, Dodona had become the holiest of shrines in Greece. Zeus, the god of the grove, spoke to people through the sound of leaves, as these were rustled by the birds. Eventually, the subtle sounds of leaves and wind were drowned by the noise of pilgrims, who came to Dodona in increasing numbers. Priests said that the voice of the god might be heard instead through the sound of balls suspended over a basin, when wind knocked the spheres against the rim.

Herodotus believed that the two black doves were Egyptian priestesses that had been sold into slavery. They were called 'black' because of their complexions and 'doves' because their language sounded like the cries of birds. Corvids, however, are capable of a remarkable range of vocalizations and were famed even in antiquity for their ability to mimic human speech. They are also universally associated with prophecy, so it is likely that they inspired the oracle of Dodona.

Birds in general were associated with divination in the cultures of Greece and Rome, and crows were perhaps second only to eagles in importance. In the final book of Homer's *Iliad*, King Priam prays for a favourable omen before going to negotiate the ransom of the body of his son Hector, slaughtered by Achilles. Immediately, an enormous 'black eagle' appeared, and the monarch knew that his mission would not be in vain. The designation 'eagle' (*aquila*) was used loosely for large birds of prey, including hawks and vultures. No common eagle is entirely black, and the 'black eagle' was probably a raven.

Crows – probably hooded crows – were most especially known as symbols of auspicious marriage. At Rhodian weddings people would sing 'the crow song' in the hope that the couple would be faithful and have their union blessed with children:

> Kind sirs, give a handful of wheat to the Crow
> The child of Apollo, or a platter of wheat,
> Or a loaf or a penny, or what you will . . .[1]

The singing was a custom similar to our modern carolling, and children probably sometimes sang the song in return for a treat.

Accordingly, crows were sacred to Hera, the goddess of marriage, as later to her Roman equivalent Juno. In *The Voyage of Argo* by Apollonius Rhodes, written in the third century BC, Jason, the hero, faced seemingly impossible tasks in his quest to obtain the Golden Fleece. The goddesses Athena, Aphrodite and Hera came to his aid by making the powerful sorceress Medea fall in love with the young man. A short time later Jason was walking with Mopsus, the master of divination, beside a poplar tree that was a favourite roost for crows. One of the birds, sent by Hera, said to Mopsus: 'Who is this inglorious seer who has not the sense to realize what even children know, that a girl does not permit herself to say a single word of love to a young man who brings an escort with him? Off with you, foolish prophet' (book III, lines 923–51). Mopsus immediately understood that Hera had arranged for Medea and Jason to meet alone, and he cheerfully withdrew. With the help of Medea, Jason was able to elude the dragon that guarded the Golden Fleece and escape with the prize to his ship.

The ambivalence of Graeco-Roman culture regarding crows is especially clearly expressed in Aelian. He wrote that crows in an erotic partnership love one another intensely and never indulge in promiscuous intercourse. If one crow should die, the other would never take another mate. But a single crow at a wedding, for that very reason, was an ill omen, suggesting that either the bride or groom would soon die.

According to legends and fables, corvids do not seem to have been on very good terms with the gods, since they were notorious for stealing meat that had been left on altars. According to one Aesopian fable, told by the Greek Babrius, a sick raven told his mother to pray to the gods for his recovery. She replied that none of the gods was likely to help her son, since he had robbed them of all their sacrificial offerings.

The peacock eventually displaced the crow in the favour of Hera. In one popular fable first told by the Roman Phaedrus, a jackdaw picked up some feathers of a peacock to adorn himself. He then, scorning his own kind, tried to join a flock of peacocks.

The birds immediately attacked him, stripped away the feathers and pecked the poor jackdaw until he flew away. He tried to rejoin the other jackdaws, but they would no longer accept him. Many versions of the fable append a moral that one ought not to aspire above one's station in life.

The crow was sacred to Apollo, god of the sun and of music, who once took the form of a crow or hawk when the gods fled to Egypt in order to hide from the monster Typhon. Nevertheless, the relations between Apollo and crows do not generally seem to have been very harmonious. The Greek word for crow, *corone*, comes from the name of a maiden who became the mistress of Apollo. According to the version of her story told by Apollodorus, Coronis, as she was called, made love to Apollo but married a young man named Ischys. The crow, which was then white, brought the news of the marriage to Apollo. The god turned the crow black out of anger, perhaps by flaring up so that the feathers of the bird were burned. Apollo then burned Coronis to death, but he rescued the child in her womb, who was to become the great healer Asclepios. The story attempts to explain the dual aspect of the crow as a bird of the morning, whose cry greets the sun, with plumage the colour of night.

The fact that the crow bears the maiden's name suggests that in earlier versions of the tale she herself was turned into a crow. It is important to note that she is killed not simply for having an affair but for marriage with a mortal. Perhaps, then, the Greeks might at one time have thought of a mated pair of crows as Coronis and Ischys. At any rate, this is one of the earliest tales of a maiden marrying a person of lower station for love in preference to a political marriage for status and power.

Ovid in his Fasti told another story in which the god of the sun was not satisfied with his corvid servant. When Apollo was

The raven, originally white, is turned black by Apollo for bringing unwelcome news. From a mid-17th-century French edition of Ovid's *Metamorphoses*.

preparing a feast for Jupiter, the god sent a raven to gather water from a spring. The raven took a bowl and flew into the air, when it caught sight of a fig tree filled with fruit. The raven swooped down, tasted the figs, and found they were still unripe. It sat there and waited until the figs were ready, ate its fill, then thought of its duty to the god. It picked up a water snake and flew back to Apollo, saying that the serpent had blocked the stream. Apollo saw through the lie, and declared that the raven should henceforth drink no water from a spring until figs have ripened on the trees; that is why the raven speaks with a voice harsh from thirst. Apollo then placed the raven, bowl and snake in the zodiac to remind people of the bird's folly.

A few Greek legends, however, made Coronis a companion of Athena, the goddess of wisdom and of war. The Roman geographer Pausanius reported in his *Guide to Greece* that in the Greek city of Corone stood a statue of Athena holding, in her outstretched hand, not the usual owl but a crow. An alternate version of the story of Coronis, retold by Ovid in his *Metamorphoses*, made her a beautiful young woman who had many suitors. The god of the sea became infatuated with her, but she refused his advances. When the god began to pursue her, the maiden prayed to Minerva, the Roman equivalent of Athena. Suddenly the girl found herself soaring above the earth, for the goddess had changed her into a crow.

Most authors, however, told of an enmity between the crow and Athena. According to one tale, the goddess had visited the workshop of Hephaestus, blacksmith to the gods, who then attempted to rape her. Athena had fended off the advances but noticed, to her disgust, that her assailant had left some semen on one of her legs. She wiped it away with a scrap of wool, which she then threw to the ground. The semen impregnated Mother Earth, who gave birth to the child Erichthonius. Athena hid the child in a covered basket, which she entrusted to three sisters. The eldest girl became curious and opened the basket, to find, to her horror, a child with snakes around its body. The crow reported what happened to Athena, who has been angry with her ever since. Perhaps the tale alludes to the call of the crow as an announcement of morning, uncovering the mysteries of the night.

In one Aesopian fable, a crow offered a sacrifice to the goddess Athena and invited a dog to his banquet. The dog remarked that the sacrifice would be useless, since the deity detested the crow in any case. The crow replied, 'I know she does not like me, but I sacrifice so that she may be reconciled to me.'[2] Just as they would eat sacrifices to the gods, so crows and ravens might also eat the fallen bodies of men. One Greek fable told of a man going off to war, who heard the harsh calls of ravens. He froze out of fear, turned to the birds and said, 'You can croak as loud as you like, but you aren't going to make a meal of me.'[3] In the comedy *The Birds* by Aristophanes, one character uses the phrase 'Go to the ravens!' (line 28). The phrase is the origin of that well-known curse – 'Go to the dogs!' – which once had a far more specific meaning than it does today. It meant to die unattended, for canids and corvids would eat the corpses of those who were not buried promptly.

But people could not help noticing that, without much aid from either gods or men, crows seemed to thrive in cities. The crows were also significant for the Greeks and Romans as symbols of long life. This association is not entirely fanciful, since many crows can live for twenty years or more, while ravens can live for over thirty. A passage quoted by Plutarch from a lost work of Hesiod that was entitled *The Precepts of Chiron* stated that the crow lived as long as nine generations of aged men. He added that the life of a stag was four times that of a crow, but a raven lived three times as long as a stag. If we say that the aged men lived for seventy years, a little arithmetic reveals the life of a crow as 630 years, while the raven lived a full 7,560 years.

The proverbial longevity of crows has often made them important in heraldry, as in the arms of Harry Holmes-Tarn. The Latin motto reads 'Be vigorous in eternity.'

In a delightful dialogue by Plutarch usually entitled 'On the Use of Reason by Irrational Animals', Odysseus, a man famed for his wit, tries vainly to argue the superiority of human beings in debate with a pig by the name of Gryllus. When the Greek hero claimed that humans showed a higher morality, the pig had this devastating reply: 'As for Penelope's [Odysseus's wife's] self-restraint, countless cackling crows will heap laughter and scorn on it, because any crow that loses her mate lives alone not just for a short time but for nine human generations.' Horapollo had given the life of a crow as a slightly more modest 400 years. We should remember that in an era when the life expectancy for human beings was only a bit more than twenty years, longevity was greatly valued and intimately associated with wisdom.

In the early centuries of Graeco-Roman civilization, divination by means of birds had been intuitive. The dramatic appearance of avian life at a critical moment would be a message of fate. Plutarch wrote in his life of Alexander the Great that crows or ravens had led the famous conqueror and his troops to the temple of Ammon in Egypt. The birds even called out when soldiers went astray, to lead the stragglers back to the army. Later, however, crows foretold the death of Alexander, when two flocks fought beside the walls of Babylon, and a few crows fell at his feet.

Gradually, however, prophesy became increasingly a matter of intricate rules. In the *The Comedy of Asses* by the Roman dramatist Plautus, written in the third century BC, a man faced with a difficult decision observed, 'I've got my auspices, my auguries: the birds let me steer it where I please! Woodpecker and crow on the left, raven and barn owl on the right. "Go ahead," they say!'[4] About two centuries later Romans had become increasingly sceptical, and Cicero somewhat rhetorically asked in *De Divinatione*

(On Divination) why a raven flying to the right was a favourable omen, while a crow flying to the left was a sign of bad luck.

There are plenty of references in early Greek literature to corvids, but it is impossible to know for sure just which species are meant. The Greeks themselves probably did not even attempt to use the designations consistently, at least not until Aristotle first attempted to study animals scientifically. The word *korone* is generally translated as 'crow', while *korax* is translated as 'raven'. These are also the meanings of the two words in Greece today. In his *Historia Animalium*, Aristotle refers to the *korone* as being partially grey, which suggests he had the hooded crow (*Corvus corone cornix*) in mind. But what, then, of the carrion crow, which Aristotle does not seem to mention? Its range does not include Greece, but travellers must surely have been familiar with the bird.

Aristotle also stated that both raven (that is, *korax*) and crow (that is, *korone*) were birds that preferred to live in towns. Both might have been attracted by scraps left by human beings, not only in sacrifices but also waste. Today as in antiquity, ravens and crows are able to thrive, a bit like rodents, in urban and suburban settings. Crows may be found in any small area of grass and trees, and they show remarkable ingenuity in pecking open garbage bags. Ravens are found in metropolitan areas as well, though few people are aware of them. They are shy of human beings, but the high buildings resemble their mountainous habitat, and they often make their nests on rooftops. It is unlikely that ravens could have avoided human contact amid the smaller buildings of ancient Greece. Probably, the word *korax* often designated not only the raven but also the carrion crow and perhaps the rook, all of which are black.

Aristotle's *Historia Animalium* was the first scientific book of zoology, and, for the most part, it was remarkably accurate, though it did contain fables such as the idea that goats go blind after being sucked by nightjars. The author accurately observed that crows look after their chicks far longer than most birds, and the bond between parents and children continues even after the chicks have learned to fly.

The language of the book, however, was far more colourfully metaphoric than that of contemporary scientists. Aristotle thought of different species almost as human kingdoms, with their alliances and enmities. The crow, Aristotle observed, though a friend of the heron, was an enemy of the owl. The crow would eat the eggs of the owl at midday, when the owl could not see well, while the owl would eat the eggs of the crow by night. Contemporary ornithologists have confirmed that crows and owls do sometimes attack one another, though the exaggerated description by Aristotle would later inspire storytellers at least as much as scientists.

Roman tomb in which the wish for peaceful rest in the life to come is represented by a traditional bucolic scene showing crows pecking grapes.

Romans at times thought of animals, including corvids, with a greater fondness. Pliny wrote 'Let us also pay due gratitude to the ravens,'[5] and went on to tell the story of a raven that was hatched on the roof of the temple dedicated to Castor and Pollux. It flew down to the shop of a cobbler, where the proprietor welcomed the bird as an emissary of the gods. Living among humans, the raven soon began to talk. It would fly every day to the forum and salute the Emperor Tiberius by name; then it would greet his generals and the public. The shop where the raven lived became so popular that the proprietor of a rival establishment killed the bird in anger. Outraged citizens killed the perpetrator. The raven was given a magnificent funeral attended by a vast crowd. A flute-player led the way and Ethiopian slaves solemnly carried the covered bier on their shoulders.

Poets of Rome looked back nostalgically to an imagined age when human beings, uncorrupted by greed, lived in harmony with the elements. In Virgil's *Georgics*, probably the most famous expression of this romantic longing, the author wrote fondly of the croaking raven as presaging rain. In his life of the Roman emperor Domitian, Suetonius wrote that a crow perched on the highest point of the Capitoline Hill and 'Not being able to say "It is well," said "It will be" (*erit*).'[6] People understood this to mean that better times would come soon. The prophecy proved accurate, as Domitian, who had grown increasingly dissolute and cruel, was soon killed; a series of more benevolent rulers suceeded him.

The cry of the raven was understood by the Romans as *cras*, Latin for 'tomorrow', and was interpreted as an expression of eternal hope. The Roman poet Tibullus, a sort of early troubadour, had written, 'Ere now I would have ended my miseries in death, but fond Hope keeps the spark alive, whispering ever tomorrow things will mend.'[7] Although the author made

Roman relief showing Mithras, 'the unconquerable sun', sacrificing a great bull to rejuvenate the world as a raven looks on.

no explicit mention of the bird, the call 'tomorrow' (*cras*) seemed to make the raven a personification of hope (*spes*).

Romans found the linguistic abilities of magpies even more impressive than those of crows and ravens. Pliny wrote that certain magpies not only repeat favourite words but love them and constantly ponder their meanings. Should a magpie fail to comprehend such a word, it may die of disappointment. If the raven was a warrior, the magpie was a dedicated scholar.

As the Romans absorbed the cultures of conquered peoples, the lore of animals such as crows became increasingly varied and complex. Pliny told of a man by the name of Crates Monoceros who went into the forest with ravens perched on his shoulders and the crest of his helmet, birds which he used for falconry. The learned Roman also reported that the soul of a man named Aristeas was seen flying out of his mouth in the form of a raven as he slept.

In archaic Persian religion – where the raven had been an incarnation of Verethragna, the god of victorious battles – raven feathers were a popular talisman. The brotherhood of 'Ravens' later became the first of seven initiations in the religion of Mithras, originally from Persia, which was especially popular among soldiers and became the major rival to

Christianity in the last centuries of the Roman Empire. Mithras was known as the 'unconquerable sun', and he was widely identified with Apollo. Among other things, Mithras shared the Graeco-Roman solar deity's association with the crows. In secret ceremonies, people dressed up as ravens and lions would dance around an underground altar. Mithras was to slaughter a great bull at the end of time, in order to regenerate the earth. A dog would lap the bull's blood, a scorpion would grasp the bull's genitals, a serpent would bite the bull, and the raven, placed between Mithras and the sun, would look on. The sacrifice of the bull would nourish life, and sometimes grain was shown sprouting from the blood of the bull. Once scorned for stealing from altars, the raven had outlived the old divinities to become an attendant of God.

Roman relief showing Mithras looking over his shoulder at a raven as he prepares to sacrifice a bull and regenerate the world. This representation is unusual in showing not one raven but two, perhaps to suggest fecundity.

three

The European Middle Ages and Renaissance

Or else you'll surely hang says he, and after that, Jim Jones
It's high upon the gallows tree the crows will pick your bones.
Anonymous, 'Jim Jones in Botany Bay'

THE ROMAN HISTORIAN Livy, who was himself of Celtic descent, reported that once a huge Gaul entered a camp of the Roman army and challenged any man to single combat. Most of the soldiers were intimidated by the size and boldness of the stranger, but a young tribune named Marcus Valerius accepted. As the fighting was about to begin, a raven landed on the helmet of Valerius and looked at the Gaul. When the two opponents approached within striking range, the raven rose and attacked the Gaul, beating the man with his wings, tearing him with talons, and driving him to panic. Soon the challenger was killed, and the raven flew off to the east. Since they were confident that some deity had sent the bird, the Romans rallied and won the ensuing battle. The tribune assumed the name of Valerius Corvus – 'Valerius the Crow'.

What deity could have sent the raven? The crow was, as we have seen, sometimes associated with Juno, Minerva and Apollo, but never in connection with battles. To send such a bird of battle would, however, have been completely in character for several Celtic deities, especially the Irish goddesses of battle, Badbh and Morrigan. A Celtic helmet of iron from the second or third century BC, found in Ciumeşti, Romania, is topped by an image of a raven with hinged wings. These would flap as the wearer entered battle. They could even have been mistaken for a real bird, much like that on the helmet of the Roman tribune. The story of Valerius Corvus is probably a Celtic tale that was eventually adopted by the Romans. The Roman army consisted largely of foreigners, who might eventually be granted citizenship for their service. It could well be that Valerius himself was actually a Celt.

The Romans took a lot more than simply soldiers from conquered peoples. Though they produced an extensive literature, there was always a spiritual void in Roman culture. This impelled the Roman Empire to constantly expand, but it also drove the Romans to adapt the religious practices of conquered peoples – including the Egyptians, Greeks, Persians and Celts – as their own. The Celtic goddess Epona was even depicted on Roman coins riding a horse sidesaddle. The Romans, like the Greeks, generally thought of the Celts and Germans as barbarians, but the Romans also admired the vitality of those supposedly primitive peoples.

Decorative letters showing intertwined birds and animals from *The Book of Kells*, executed in Ireland in the late 8th or early 9th century AD. The creatures are not identifiable, although some of the birds may be ravens.

The peoples of Northern Europe may not have produced a literary culture like that of Greece and Rome, but their visual arts, featuring curvilinear designs based on forms of animals and plants, had a sensuous vividness that the more cerebral cultures of the Mediterranean seldom or never matched. For the Romans, animals were often omens and symbols, but in Celto-Germanic culture they had a more autonomous reality. They might be wise or powerful in their own right, not simply as mascots of anthropomorphic gods.

The literature that has come down to us from the Celtic and Nordic peoples was not transcribed until well into the Middle Ages, but it is filled with stories and deities that go back to archaic times. This literature, unlike that of Greece and Rome, shows little interest in abstractions, but it is emotionally very complex. Like most serious literature from the ancient world, it is tragic. Nevertheless, its tragic vision is almost always leavened by humour, especially in Irish literature. The archaic literature of Northern Europe blends gritty realism, extravagant magic and satiric exaggeration, in a manner not entirely unlike that of Irish drinking songs in more recent times.

Crows, along with elephants, are among the few animals that often seem to have a sense of humour, which contrasts with their sombre plumage. It is natural that crows should be perhaps the most complex and interesting animals in these colourful tales. In the sagas of the Vikings, Celts and Saxons, crows and ravens are almost always lurking somewhere in the background, and their ominous calls are heard at important moments.

The raven or crow was particularly associated with Odin, the supreme god of the Vikings, who was sometimes known as 'Lord of the Ravens'. He had two ravens – named 'Hugin' (thought) and 'Munin' (memory) – which perched on his

Decorative letters showing interlaced birds in *The Book of Kells*.
Although the elongated bodies of these creatures suggests swans,
their heads resemble those of ravens.

shoulders. In 'Grimnir's Sayings', from the Nordic *Poetic Edda*,
Odin visited Geirrod, king of the Goths, disguised in a blue
cloak, to test the monarch's reputation for flouting the laws
of hospitality. Geirrod arrested Odin and suspended the god

from a tree between two fires. As he was tortured, Odin told of heaven and earth, and he said:

Hugin and Munin fly every day over the wide world;
I fear for Hugin that he will not come back,
Yet I tremble more for Munin.[1]

This was the fear that the world would degenerate into chaos, as reflection and recollection, the gifts of civilization, are lost. The torture of Odin suggests a shamanic initiation, where the subject is granted access to arcane knowledge. Odin, who was the god of magic as well as of war, may originally have been a shaman, while the ravens and wolves that accompany him may have been animal helpers.

Perhaps even more than for the Greeks and Romans, ravens became birds of omen for the Vikings. A raven croaking in front of a home might foretell the death of the householder. A raven with wings outstretched became the standard of Viking chiefs going into battle. The medieval *Saga of Flokki* tells of how a mariner discovered Iceland by releasing a raven and sailing after it.

Crows and ravens had a similar importance for the early Celts. Lugh, whose name means 'shining one', was the Celtic god of light. The name is related to the Gaulish word lugos, which can mean 'raven'. This suggests that at one point Lugh may have been, like Odin, a god of ravens, and he also shared with Odin an association with battles and with sorcery. In the Irish *Book of Invasions*, ravens warned Lugh of the approach of his enemies the Formians. The original name for the city of Lyon, *Lugdunum*, means 'Raven's Hill', so called because the flight of ravens showed the original settlers where to build.

But the Celtic imagery of ravens and crows is generally more chthonic than solar. Numerous ravens have been found buried in pits by Celts during the Iron Age, and one in England at Winklebury, Wiltshire, was deliberately arranged with wings outstretched at the bottom of a hole, suggesting that it may have been part of a ritual sacrifice. Corvids are, as already mentioned, most frequently associated with the battle goddesses Badbh and Morrigan. Both had the ability to take triple form, and their appearance before or during a battle usually foretold doom. In the old Irish saga *The Death of Cu Culainn*, the mythic hero Cu Culainn encounters three crow-like hags, probably a

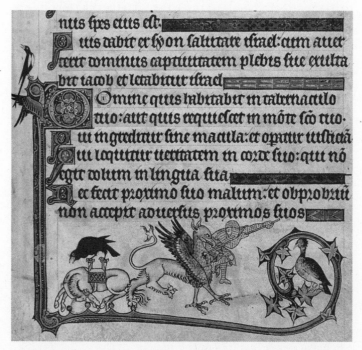

Illustration of a crow in the *Alphonso Psalter* (13th century). Although beautifully painted, the birds in this Psalter seem oddly static, perhaps because the artist sought to depict scenes in the perspective of eternity.

manifestation of Badbh, on his way into battle, and they trick him into violating a taboo by eating the meat of a dog. Cu Culainn is mortally wounded soon after, and he ties himself to a tree in order to die on his feet. His enemies watch from afar, afraid to approach him, until a crow or raven, Badbh, alights on his shoulder.

The Welsh tales in the *Mabinogion* are only a bit closer to the world of chivalry. In 'The Dream of Rhonabwy', the chieftains Arthur and Owein match wits in a board game rather like chess, while their entourages engage in battle. Arthur was accompanied by his knights; Owein's companions were magical ravens, able to recover from wounds and even rise from the dead. The ravens were close to defeating the men of Arthur, when the rulers ended their contest and declared a peace.

In the story 'Branwen, Daughter of Lly^r', the hero is the giant Brân, whose name in Welsh means 'crow' or 'raven'. His sister Branwen, whose name means 'white crow', married an Irish chieftain, but was abused by her husband. She sent a starling across the sea with news of her mistreatment, and the armies of Brân soon invaded Ireland. After a terrible battle, Brân and his men killed every person in Ireland except for five pregnant women who had taken refuge in a cave. Brân himself was mortally wounded, while only six of his followers survived. At the command of the giant, his men cut off his head, which continued to speak, and the warriors carried the head back to London. They finally buried it in the Tower of London, and, according to legend, the ravens in the Tower are the spirit of Brân. As long as ravens do not disappear from there, Britain can never be successfully invaded.

People looked to animals less for prophecy, as they had in the ancient world, and more as purveyors of moral lessons or

Crows and other birds in the Cocharelli *Tractatus de vitiis septem* (late 14th century). The Middle Ages has often been stereotyped as 'otherworldly', but the artist who painted these birds obviously took keen delight in observing nature.

objects of aesthetic contemplation. In a famous scene in the story 'Peredur, Son of Efrawg', also from the *Mabinogion,* the hero Peredur came across a raven that was eating a duck in the snow, and he began to dream of his beloved. The whiteness of the snow reminded him of her skin, while the blackness of the raven was like her hair, and two drops of blood were like the redness of her cheeks. This image, with variations, was to be repeated with variations many times in folk literature, for example in Wolfram von Eschenbach's knightly epic *Parzifal* and the Grimm Brothers' fairy tale 'Little Snow White'. This scene sums up all the beauty and cruelty that we have come to associate with the Middle Ages.

The Middle Ages may be closer to us in time than the Graeco-Roman world, but medieval times are, in many ways, the more mysterious. The figures on Grecian vases and Roman wall paintings appear clearly focused on their activities. The figures in medieval paintings, by contrast, usually stare straight out at us, the viewers, with stern if slightly melancholy eyes. Artists of the Middle Ages and Renaissance often painted several scenes from a

Medieval English woodcut illustrating the *Fables* of Aesop, showing a contest of wills between the fox and the crow, two notoriously clever animals.

story in a single painting, reminding us that they represented part of the eternal condition.

In bestiaries of the Middle Ages, animals were primarily allegorical, created by the Almighty to illustrate moral lessons for human beings. Thus the stag and elephant might symbolize Christ, while the serpent and pig could represent the Devil. But medieval authors often simply delighted in telling stories about animals. As Europe converted to Christianity, the demise of the anthropomorphic pagan deities sometimes allowed an even more archaic heritage to re-emerge. The folk Christianity of medieval Europe was often less anthropocentric than the religions of Greece and Rome. Animals in medieval literature often appear not simply as emissaries of anthropomorphic beings, as they often did among the Greeks and Romans, but as active participants in the stories of men and women.

As medieval people adapted the lore of earlier times to Christianity, they often added a moralistic gloss. Corvids, however, emerged as both good and evil, even, like Yahweh of the Old Testament, as both at once. Authors might extol crows in one passage and curse them relentlessly in the next. Hugh of Fouilloy's *Aviarium*, written in the early to mid-twelfth century but published nearly 300 years later, stated that 'the raven is understood sometimes as a preacher, sometimes a sinner, sometimes the Devil.'[2] Perhaps because ravens suggested a combination of good and evil, French peasants used to say that corrupt priests would become ravens and bad nuns, crows.

Crows and ravens were especially closely associated with death. Every warrior, at least until historically very recent times, knew that a possible destiny for him was to be eaten by crows. This was especially disturbing in those cultures where the fate of the deceased in the next world was believed to be at least

In this 19th-century illustration by Wilhelm Kaulbach of the fables of Reynard the fox, the crafty protagonist is taken for dead and crows arrive to peck at his body. More crows gather at the nearby gallows.

partly contingent on a proper burial. Macabre, and sometimes fanciful, details were sometimes added to accounts of scavenging crows. Medieval authors such as Isidore of Seville and Hugh of Fouilloy told that the raven would first peck out the eyes of its victim and then extract the brain through the sockets. Konrad von Megenberg, in his popular natural history published in 1349, reported that ravens would deliberately peck out the eyes of mules or oxen on a farm. The peasants, seeing the domestic animals were of no further use, would then kill and skin them. The clever ravens would, in this way, get a chance to devour part of the carcasses.

The idea of being eaten by animals at times arouses a very primeval terror. Being left as a corpse for crows and ravens can mean, in other words, being abandoned and cast out from human society. This was the fate of criminals, whose bodies were left out on the gallows as a public display. It was graphically expressed in the Anglo-Saxon epic *Beowulf*, written some time between the middle of the seventh and the end of the tenth centuries AD:

> It was like the misery felt by an old man who has lived to see his son's body swing on the gallows. He begins to keen and weep for his boy, watching the raven gloat where he hangs . . .[3]

Warnings against a life of crime often invoked the fate of being eaten by crows and ravens. The chopping block on which criminals were beheaded came to be known as the 'ravenstone'.

In many popular ballads, some of which may go back to the Middle Ages or before, ravens or crows looked out over a battlefield and plan to devour a slain knight. An anonymous ballad, 'The Twa Corbies', from the Scottish–English Border region, runs:

> As I was walking all alane,
> I heard twa corbies making a mane:
> The tane [*the one*] unto the tither did say,
> 'What sall we gang [*where shall we go*] and dine the day?'
>
> 'In behint yon auld fail dyke [*turf ditch*]
> I wot there lies a new-slain knight;
> And naebody kens [*nobody knows*] that he lies there
> But his hawk, his hound, and his lady fair.
>
> 'His hound is to the hunting gane,
> His hawk to fetch the wild-fowl hame,
> His lady's t'en anither mate,
> So we may mak' our dinner sweet.

'Ye'll sit on his white hause-bane, [*neck-bone*]
And I'll pike out his bonny blue e'en
Wi' ae lock o' his gowden hair
We'll theek [*thatch*] our nest when it grows bare.

'Mony a one for him maks mane,
    but nane sall ken [*none shall know*] whar he is gane:
O'er his white banes, when they are bare,
The wind sall blaw [*shall blow*] for evermair.'[4]

In other versions of the ballad, the faithful lady and hound keep watch over the knight's body and protect it from the crows or ravens.

In Shakespeare's play *Julius Caesar* (v, i), the rebel Cassius has a premonition of his defeat and says:

. . . ravens, crows and kites
Fly o'er our heads and downward look at us,
As we were sickly prey: their shadows seem
A canopy most fatal, under which
Our army lies, ready to give up the ghost.

These words echo in the last speeches of the play, where Octavian and Mark Antony declare that the defeated Brutus at least is to be given a decent burial.

From the end of the Middle Ages to the modern period, depicting a flock of crows perched around the gallows became a convention in the visual arts, but there was one interesting exception. Crows were never shown gathered around the body of the crucified Christ or, for that matter, those of the two thieves that were executed with him. They were also virtually never shown picking at the bodies of martyrs, even though martyrdom was often depicted in gory detail. Had crows been shown in that capacity, the birds would certainly have been demonized or glorified. As it was, they were usually respected, which is generally much safer for any sort of creature.

In 1562 the Flemish painter Pieter Bruegel the Elder completed a canvas usually entitled *The Triumph of Death*, which

Crow pecking at the eyes of a dead soldier in a late 13th-century English *Apocalypse*. Crows assembling on the battlefields and devouring the slain became an increasingly familiar sight in the late Middle Ages as wars increased in both frequency and scale.

contained a skeletal figure holding an hourglass in one hand and a bell in the other, riding a horse that draws a cart filled with skulls. Several people, perhaps weakened by hunger and plague, are being crushed under the wheels of the advancing cart. Also on the horse, directly behind the emaciated rider, is a large crow or raven, looking down at the dying and the dead.

Numerous European superstitions make crows and ravens avatars of death. If a single crow flies three times over a roof or perches on it, that is a sign that the person inside will soon die. In East Yorkshire, England, people say that if a crow perches in a churchyard somebody will be buried there before a year has passed. Ravens are particularly ominous; if one croaks near the house of a sick person, that person does not have long to live.

Emaciated figures representing Death drive a horse and cart filled with skulls over the bodies of hapless men and women in Pieter Bruegel the Elder's *The Triumph of Death*, 1562. Note their 'familiar' perched on the horse.

One late medieval manuscript now in the Bodleian Library in Oxford tells how the people of London had suffered three years of plague, when, in about 1474,

> there bred a raven on Charing Cross in London; and never had one seen breed there before. And after that there came a great death of pestilence, that lasted three years; and people died mightily in every place, man, woman and child.[5]

There was another allusion to the superstition that ravens can foretell death in Shakespeare's *Othello, the Moor of Venice* (IV, i), when the hero says:

> O, it comes o'er my memory
> As doth the raven o'er the infected house
> Boding to all . . .

In Shakespeare's *Macbeth* (I, v), Lady Macbeth observes while planning the murder of King Duncan:

> The raven himself is hoarse
> That croaks the fatal entrance of Duncan
> Under my battlements . . .

But we should remember that, although the raven may have been a messenger of doom, it seldom seemed to be the *cause* of misfortune.

Death was far more familiar to people of the Middle Ages and Renaissance than it is to people of today. Life expectancy was lower, not least because there was comparatively little protection against famine or disease. Almost the entire population of Europe was rural, and people grew up seeing chickens and pigs slaughtered for food. For those who could expect, or at least hope for, eternal bliss, death was not necessarily a bad thing. It was imposing in its solemn grandeur, as a culmination of a person's life. Furthermore, death was not regarded as a private matter but, far more, as a public affair. People wished to know in advance the hour of their death, so they might prepare for it. They wished to die in bed surrounded by family, friends, and perhaps even old enemies with whom they could exchange forgiveness. Nobody wished to be taken unexpectedly by death and thus deprived of the chance to make peace with God and the world. The announcement by a raven of imminent death might be frightening, but it was still often felt as a blessing.

As we have already seen, Romans understood the cry of a raven or crow as *cras*, meaning 'tomorrow'. As virulent plagues and increasingly brutal wars began to sweep across Europe at the end of the Middle Ages, this call came to be understood as a reminder of mortality. At the same time, the call was an emblem of the

In an illustration by the young Albrecht Dürer for Sebastian Brandt's *The Ship of Fools* (1400), a fool is charmed by the ravens' croaking *cras, cras* (*tomorrow, tomorrow*), persuading him to procrastinate.

Medieval illustration to *The Book of the City of Ladies* (1405) by
Christine de Pisan. It shows the sibyl Amalthea, who led Aeneas
on his journey to the Underworld. She received her gift of
prophecy from Apollo, and here she gestures towards two
prophetic birds – a raven and a hooded crow.

procrastinator, often the person who would complacently put
off making his peace with God, not realizing that he could die
at any moment.

With the revival of pagan learning in the Renaissance, the crow
became a symbol of the maiden Pandora. According to a Greek
myth first told by Hesiod, she had opened a box containing all
the evils of the world. When she realized what had happened,
she slammed the lid shut, but only Hope remained in the bottom
of the box. As the extreme pessimism of the late Middle Ages
and early Renaissance began to give way to an ideal of progress,
people began to view the maiden less as a symbol of sin than of
fallible humanity. The corvid call of *cras* or 'tomorrow' seemed

to resonate more optimistically, and artists sometimes painted a crow on the box or shoulder of Pandora.

The association of crows with mortality is still with us in the expression 'crow's feet', meaning lines of age around the eyes. The term probably goes back to the use of a crow's foot in magic spells. The connection of crows with prophesy is reflected in the term 'crow's nest', meaning the observation tower near the top of a ship's mast. The expression comes in part from the crow's habit of building its nest near the top of a tree. Since, however, the sailor on watch in the crow's nest endeavours to see land or distant ships, he is a bit like a clairvoyant – that is, a crow.

Several medieval legends echoed the story of the biblical Elijah by making crows or ravens the envoy of God. Jacob de Voragine, for example, told in *The Golden Legend* how St Paul the Hermit once took refuge in a forest cave in order to escape the Emperor Decius. Every day a crow brought him half a loaf of bread. Once, however, St Paul was visited by St Anthony, and the crow brought an entire loaf.

The crow was often depicted with St Vincent. Jacob de Voragine tells of how the Emperor Dacian ordered the body of the martyred St Vincent to be left in an open field and devoured by scavengers. A band of angels first appeared around the body so that no beast or bird could approach. Then a crow flew down and attacked the other birds, some larger than itself, and drove

This coat of arms takes an optimistic view of the raven's proverbial call of *cras* or 'tomorrow'. James Aitken's motto reads 'Happy today; tomorrow three times more'.

The crow is not an exalted animal in Christian iconography, but Diego Velázquez's *St Anthony Abbot and St Paul the Hermit with Raven* of *c.* 1635 shows one apparently descending directly from Heaven, like the Holy Spirit.

A raven brings a loaf of bread to the two hermits in Albrecht Dürer's woodcut *St Anthony and St Paul in the Wilderness*, 1504.

them all away. A wolf approached, but the crow, cawing and pecking, chased away that animal too. Finally, the crow turned toward the body and gazed intently in wonder. We could understand this mysterious crow as a symbol of Christ, though it seems rather more pagan than Christian.

In Islam people took a far more negative view of crows. One popular legend told that on one occasion Mohammed was hiding in a cave to escape his enemies, when a crow, then a white bird, caught sight of him. The crow shouted 'Ghar! Ghar!' – that is, 'Cave! Cave!' – in an attempt to betray the prophet. The armed men, however, failed to comprehend and walked past the entrance to the cavern. When Mohammed left his refuge he turned the crow black and cursed it, saying that from that day on the crow must forever repeat the treacherous cry.

The thirteenth-century Arab encyclopaedist Hamdullah Al- Mustaufa Al-Qazwini of Iraq wrote in his treatise on animals that the crow was one of the 'five scoundrels' among animals, the others being the mad dog, the serpent, the rat and the kite.[6] Muslims were prohibited from hunting or killing animals while on pilgrimage to Mecca. These animals, however, were considered so noxious that an exception was made for them. Believers were obligated to destroy such vermin under any circumstances. Al-Qazwini, however, suggested so many charms and medicines that could be made from the bodies of corvids that the reader might wonder if they were really killed simply out of obligation. Maybe they were killed for the wonders that could be performed with their bodies. The spleen of a crow, for example, acted as a love charm for anybody who hung it on his body. The fat of a rook, when mixed with the oil of roses and rubbed on one's cheeks, would make the Sultan grant any request. For those who liked to stir up trouble, the eye of a crow or rook and one of an owl, if mixed together and burned, would cause a feud to break out in a group of people.

Jewish perspectives on the crow during the Middle Ages and Renaissance were also generally negative. The legendary Rabbi Isaac Luria of Egypt developed a theory of transmigration of souls, similar to that of several Asian religions, in which a being might go through many incarnations on the way to redemption. His followers sometimes claimed that those who were callous towards the poor might be reincarnated as crows. Moses Galante of Safed reported that Rabbi Luria had once identified two ravens as the souls of the biblical figures Balak and Balaam. Yet another crow was, allegedly according to Luria, the reincarnation of a hated tax collector. Nevertheless, crows were far too familiar a part of daily life for Jews, or anybody else, to regard them in either consistently negative or positive terms. In an era before

A chough is a corvid that closely resembles a true crow and has often been mistaken for one. According to some Welsh legends, King Arthur lives on as a chough.

portable timepieces, when people generally marked time largely by the calls and behaviour of animals, Jews would begin their Sabbath when crows settled down for the night.

In Britain, a totemic regard for corvids probably survived longer than in any other part of Europe, though this was stripped of its original mythological context. Pierre Belon reported in *L'Histoire de la Nature des Oyseaux* (first published 1555) that it was forbidden in England under penalty of a heavy fine to do any harm to ravens. The reason given by Belon was that if the ravens did not consume carrion, the meat would putrefy and poison the air. We might call the reason 'ecological', but the English probably thought of it in very practical terms. They were intuitively aware of a connection between decaying flesh and disease, but they wished, above all, to avoid unpleasant sights and smells.

Writing about half a century after Belon, however, Miguel de Cervantes of Spain offered another explanation of the English prohibition against killing ravens in his celebrated novel *Don Quixote de la Mancha*. The hero explained that King Arthur of Britain had been transformed into a raven and his people awaited his return. They would not kill a raven for fear it might be the legendary king. Folklorists have confirmed that this belief persisted in Wales and Cornwall at least to the last decades of the nineteenth century. In some versions of the legend, the king had become a chough. The story probably reflected some lingering veneration of the crow as a totem animal.

There was an odd sort of parallelism in lore of the Middle Ages and Renaissance between the symbolism of the sacred and the profane, and very often the same object or creature might symbolize both qualities. Accordingly, an apple was a symbol of the Fall when it was placed in the hand of Eve. When placed in the hand of Mary, 'the new Eve', the apple became a symbol of redemption. In a similar way, the crow or raven might represent extremes of good or evil, depending on the context in which it appeared. In the presence of St Vincent, the raven was an avatar of God, but when accompanying a witch it was an emissary of the Devil.

The association of crows with witchcraft was in part a repudiation of their archaic use in augury. Bestiaries of the Middle Ages, which often sound very superstitious to us today, stated emphatically that crows should not be regarded as portents of the future. Edward Topsell, an English zoologist of the mid-seventeenth century, stated, 'It is great wickedness to believe that God communicateth his counsels to crows.'[7] He went on to add that the divination using crows, as practised by American Indians, was actually the work of evil spirits. In their collection of German legends the Grimm brothers reported that a man and women from Lüttich were executed in 1610 for roaming about in the form of wolves, while their son of twelve accompanied them as a raven. Isobel Gowdie, a Scots woman who confessed to witchcraft in 1662, said that crows were a favourite form that witches assumed when travelling around at night.

The familiars of witches, however, were generally smaller animals than crows and ravens. William of Malmesbury has told of an English witch in Berkeley, Gloucestershire, whose favourite familiar was a jackdaw, a bird whose chattering often seems to mimic the rhythms of human speech. One day in 1065, the bird began to prattle more insistently than usual. The woman dropped her knife in fear, for she realized that she was about to die. That day she did indeed become very ill, and the Devil soon carried her away.

The alchemists of the Renaissance devised complex and esoteric ways to use the chthonic powers of crows and, especially,
ravens. The Englishman Robert Fludd, writing in the early seventeenth century, called the dark sediment left in the bottom of
a retort after distillation 'raven' or 'raven's head'. This, Fludd
believed, was the primal material out of which the cosmos had
once been created. This was the dwelling of the Devil, yet it was
also the starting-point of the ascent to God. In the intricate alle-
gories of the alchemists, a raven might be identified with the
grave or with the sun under eclipse. The raven eating carrion,
even the dead bodies of human beings, signified the transformation of all things as the world, slowly but inexorably, moved
towards perfection.

four

Asia

Of men, the barber smartest is;
The jackal, of the beasts;
The crow is cleverest of birds;
The White Robe, of the priests.
The *Panchatantra* (translated by Arthur W. Ryder)

ONLY RARELY, as in the Ghost Dance Religion of the American Indians, has a major religion centred largely on the crow or raven. Corvids, however, are associated with prophecy, wisdom and longevity in most of the world. Perhaps, in very archaic times, there was a cult of the crow, which gradually spread through much of the world and now survives in fragmentary legends and folk beliefs. The geographic centre of such a cult would probably have been north-central Asia. From there it appears to have spread to the Inuit and related peoples in the east, to the Celts and Nordic peoples in the west, and, in more attenuated forms, to a vast number of other peoples from the Hebrews to the Chinese. Many anthropologists have noted a resemblance between the shamanic beliefs of Siberian peoples and those of Native Americans in the far north. Throughout the Arctic Circle and beyond, a raven or crow is sometimes celebrated as

The delicacy and transience of plum blossom, a familiar theme in Japanese art and poetry, is highlighted by the contrast with the crow in *Full Moon with Crow on Plum Branch*, 1880s, by Kawanabe Kyosai.

a creator deity. The raven is also sometimes a trickster, at once holy and obscene.

Creation myths are not the oldest products of folk traditions; they generally come in the transition from a tribal to a more cosmopolitan society. The deities who create the world are not always those who are actively worshipped, and the myths of creation often commemorate a passing era. Such creators as the Greek Gaia and the Hindu Brahma, for example, served to link current religious traditions with an even more archaic past. The several myths of creation by a raven or crow, found among peoples of the Arctic Circle, may be remnants of a lost mythology. These myths are generally fragmentary and not integrated in any well-developed religious cosmology. They are moments of illumination, a bit like the sudden appearance of a raven amid the snow.

Crow family in a Japanese print by Kōno Bairei of *c.* 1860. The female parent intently looks for food, while the male looks on nervously as the youngsters attempt perhaps their first flight.

The Chuckchee of northeastern Siberia tell that once there was only Raven and his wife, and they were bored. When his wife asked Raven to create a world, her husband replied that he did not know how. She then went to sleep and gave birth to twins, children who had no feathers and were at first amused by Raven with his croaking voice; these were the first human beings. Raven, challenged and inspired by her act, created the earth. He defecated to make mountains, rivers and valleys, and then he created animals and plants. The Inuit of Kukulik Island in the Bering Strait tell that Raven created their land by diving into the water and bringing up sand. The pebbles in the sand became human beings, and Raven taught people to hunt and fish.

In tales of the Koryak from the Kamchatka Peninsula in Siberia, Big Raven is the creator of the world and the ancestor of the tribe. Raven Man is his degenerate counterpart, who is greedy and impulsive yet powerful. In one story, Raven Man had wooed Yinyé-a-nyéut, the eldest daughter of Big Raven, but she had wedded Little Bird instead. Suddenly, everything became completely dark, and a shaman divined that Raven Man had swallowed the sun. Yinyé-a-nyéut went to Raven Man, whom she distracted with coy, flattering words. Then, suddenly, she seized him and tickled him under his arm, until Raven Man laughed and the sun escaped.

A Japanese legend also tells that once a monster prepared to devour the sun. To prevent this, the rulers of heaven created the first crow. Just as the sun was about to disappear, the crow flew straight into the monster's throat and choked it, thus saving the celestial sphere. Today, the crow claims grain from the fields as its due in return for that act of heroism, and farmers can hardly begrudge the reward.

There may perhaps be traces of an archaic corvid deity in the many legends where a crow or raven becomes an avatar of fate. The Japanese tell, for example, that the hero Jimmu-Tenno was wandering about in search of a place to found his kingdom, when he caught sight of a crow sent by the sun-goddess Amaterasu. He followed the crow to Yamato, where he settled in 660 BC, to become the ancestor of all the Japanese emperors.

The intimate association of crows and ravens with the sun is also told in the tale of the divine archer Yi, one of the most popular figures in Chinese mythology. Once there were ten suns that lived in the celestial mulberry tree beyond the ocean. These were the children of Tiayang Dijun, the lord of heaven, and Xi-he, goddess of the sun, and each day one child would ascend into the sky. One day the suns rebelled against the decrees of heaven and all ten appeared in the sky at a single time, burning crops, drying up seas and even melting glaciers. The legendary Confucian emperor Yao prayed to Tiayang Dijun for help, and the god sent Yi with his arrows to frighten the suns into returning to their tree. Yi, however, decided that he had no choice but to shoot the suns. With each arrow that he shot, a great ball of fire would appear in the sky and a raven with three legs would fall to the ground. Yao feared that, if Yi were not stopped, the world would be left in darkness, so he stole one arrow from the archer's quiver, and thus the last sun was spared. Chinese sculptures of the Han dynasty sometimes show a three-legged raven in the sun, the legs corresponding to dawn, noon and dusk.

In China, as throughout most of the world, crows and ravens were at least as important in local legends as in universal mythologies. One charming tale of a man who became a crow is found in the collection commonly known as *Strange Stories from a Chinese Studio*, written in the seventeenth century and attributed to P'u Sung-ling. A young man from a poor family named Yi Jung from the province of Hunan had failed to pass his examinations and was in despair, when he stopped to pray in the temple of Wu Wang, the Taoist deity of crows. Yi Jung was about to rest when an attendant came and led him into the presence of Wu Wang himself. At the command of the deity, the poor student was given a black robe. On putting on the garment, he found himself changed into a crow. He then married a crow named Chu-ch'ing, and together with her and others in their flock they caught cakes and bits of meat that the mariners threw them for good luck. Failing to heed the counsel of his wife, however, he approached

In spite of the generally negative reputation of crows in Islamic culture, story-tellers and artists admired their cleverness in the fable 'Crows Trapping Owls in a Cave'. This 14th-century illustration is from an Arabic fable collection, *Kalila wa Dimna*, a translation of the Hindu *Panchatantra*.

human beings too freely and was hit in the breast by an arrow shot by a soldier.

Yi Jung suddenly found himself in human form lying wounded on the temple floor. On recovering, he did not forget his life as a crow with Chu-ch'ing. He went back to worship at the temple, prayed to Wu Wang and left food for the crows. Later, after Yi Jung had passed his examinations, he sacrificed a sheep. This brought a flock of birds, and with them was Chu-ch'ing, who had become a river spirit. She returned the black robes to her husband, saying that should he ever wish to see her he need only put them on and fly to her home.

In the *Ramayana*, an ancient Hindu epic, Yama, the lord of death, once took the form of a crow to hide himself from the demon Ravana. On regaining his true form, Yama blessed the crow, saying that the bird would never die of age or disease, though it might still be killed. Because of this blessing, crows eat before human beings even in times of dire famine. Some Hindus leave out food for crows as an offering to Yama, in the hopes that he will be merciful to departed friends and family. But the crow in Hinduism has been an attribute not only of Yama but of Varuna, the wise king of heaven.

The owl may have a reputation for wisdom in the folklore of the West, but in India this honour goes to the crow. In both traditions the crows and owls are forever battling in an epic war, which may represent the conflict between day and night. The *Panchatantra*, a great animal epic of Hindu tradition, devotes an entire book to the conflict between crows and owls.

Once the birds assembled to elect a king and chose the owl for his venerable appearance. They were preparing a magnificent coronation, at which the owl would sit on a golden throne decorated with lions, while Brahmans would recite poetry and maidens would sing. Suddenly the crow, cleverest of birds, appeared. He laughed at the choice, saying that the owl was too ugly with his hooked beak and squinty eyes. His features

Two magpies, a design for a Japanese porcelain bowl made in the 19th century.

were without tenderness and his nature without pity. Besides, the crow explained, the birds already had a king in Garuda, the eagle-headed mount of the god Vishnu, and to take another would be an offence against heaven. The crow went on to tell many stories of those who had made foolish choices and paid the price. The other birds agreed and flew away. The owl, who had been sleeping during the day, came at evening for his coronation and learned what had happened, and owls have feuded with crows ever since.

What followed is a story of ruthless intrigue and betrayal, not unlike the wars of petty chieftains in the ancient world. A crow-king named Cloudy ruled with his court in a great banyan tree, while an owl-king named Foe-Crusher held court in a neighbouring cave. Foe-Crusher and his retinue killed every crow they encountered, until the base of the banyan tree was littered with bodies. Finally, a particularly clever crow named Live-Strong devised a plan for revenge.

In a staged fight, Cloudy reviled Live-Strong, pecked him gently, covered him with blood and flew away with his court. As the crows had planned, spies reported the fight to Foe-Crusher, who then welcomed Live-Strong as an ally. The devious crow so charmed the king of owls that he was given the choicest foods. He lived just outside the owls' cave, where he gradually built up a pile of sticks. One day, as the owls were asleep, the crows came and ignited the kindling, burning their adversaries to death.

Perhaps the most charming of all birds in the family Corvidae is the magpie, which had a reputation in both East and West for constant chattering and for stealing glittering objects. The common magpie (*Pica pica*), with sharply contrasting markings of black and white, is found through most of Eurasia and parts of the United States. The green magpie of eastern Asia (*Cissa chinensis*) is even more striking in appearance, with plumage as bright as that of a bird of paradise. For all its mischievous ways, the magpie is also a symbol of domesticity, since it builds uncommonly intricate, domed nests that hang from branches and are entered from one side. The name of the magpie in Chinese literally means 'bird of joy', and it is known as a bearer of good omens.

Above all, the magpie is a patron of lovers. One popular tale found in many versions throughout most of eastern Asia is that of the weaver maiden Zhi nu, who married a young man named Qian niu who herded oxen. The weaver maiden was the granddaughter of the Emperor of Heaven, and her task was to weave the celestial cloth with its pattern of clouds. After her marriage, Zhi nu would spend all her time laughing and frolicking with her husband, and she neglected her duties. At last, the Emperor of heaven decided that they must be separated. He placed Zhi nu in the eastern sky and Qian nu in the western sky, and between the two he set the Milky Way. Husband and wife then wept so much that there were great floods upon the earth. Finally, on the seventh day of the seventh month of the Chinese year, the magpies (in some versions, crows) flew up and formed a bridge across the sky. The weaving maiden is the star Vega and the herder is the star Altair, at opposite sides of the heavens, and every year they are reunited by the birds.

Opposite: In China the magpie is known as the 'bird of joy' and is especially associated with marital bliss.

five

Native American Culture

The earth – the crow,
The earth – the crow.
The crow brought it with him,
The crow brought it with him.

ARAPAHO INDIAN SONG

THE CROW OR RAVEN has been most prominent in the myths and legends of the far north. Part of the reason may be that the black of the crow stands out most dramatically against the snow. Part of the reason may also be that the harsh cry of the crow resonates intensely in the Arctic stillness. The most important explanation is that in the severe regions of the north, where there is seldom really enough food, the ability of the crow to survive on carrion is most feared and admired.

The Inuit and the peoples of the Northwest Coast share a cult of the crow or raven with Siberians such as the Koryak, which suggests that the legends migrated across the Bering Strait. Like Europeans before the modern period, the Native Americans have generally not distinguished sharply between the raven and crow. At any rate, the raven (as we will call the figure for convenience) seems to continually change both shape and personality in the course of adventures.

Among the Inuit, as in Europe and Asia, the raven has long had a reputation for prophetic knowledge. Inuit sometimes keep the claw of a raven as a talisman to help them in the search for food, since ravens always appear whenever an animal or human being is killed. On seeing ravens flying overhead, Inuit sometimes called to them and ask if they had seen caribou or bear. They believed (and often still do) that the ravens would dip a single wing in order to point the direction of game. Inuit say that when the soul of a shaman leaves his body to take flight, a raven may often be seen flying over his igloo.

One of the very few Inuit creation myths told of a being named Tulungusaq, who emerged out of the sky. When the swallow showed him clay at the bottom of the void, he took the form of a raven or crow in order to retrieve this primeval material, from which he then fashioned plants, animals and men. When he recovered from amazement at his creation, the raven made women to accompany the men. Finally, he made the sun and moon to relieve the primal darkness.

The Haida Indians of the Queen Charlotte Islands distinguish between two cycles of stories about Raven. In the cycle of the Greater Raven, generally recounted in solemn tones, Raven was a creator who first called the earth into being on the endless sea. This raven made human beings out of both rock and leaf, but the people of rock were never finished. The people of leaf, however, were soon ready to walk about. The Greater Raven showed people the leaf and told them that, like a leaf, they must fall and rot until there would be nothing left. In this way, death came into the world.

One legend tells that the Greater Raven had a sister, but he did not wish her to give birth to any male offspring, for fear they might challenge him. His sister had many children, and he killed

Raven design for a Kwakiutl Indian canoe.

them all. At the suggestion of Heron, the sister swallowed a burning stone, from which she was impregnated. She then gave birth to the Lesser Raven, who was robust as stone and would live forever. On seeing this, the Greater Raven gave the younger bird dominion over the world and withdrew. A variant of this myth has been found among the Athabascan Indians of northern Canada, which is probably influenced by Christianity. In a tale reminiscent of Cain and Abel, the Athabascans told of two primordial ravens, one white and the other black. The white raven created the world, but the black one was consumed with jealousy and killed his brother.

The Lesser Raven resembles Coyote, the most prominent trickster among the Indians of the southwestern United States. Both legendary figures were at once buffoon and sage, but while Coyote was known for his sexual desires, Raven was notorious for his voracious appetite. This is the destruction that is necessary for new creation in the eternal cycle of death and birth. Raven did pay a large role in the formation of the world, yet this is often as an incidental result of his trickery.

The best known of his exploits was stealing the light for the world, a story told in many variants by tribes along the Northwest Coast. The Tsimshan told that Raven had scattered fish and fruit throughout the world so that he would always have something to eat, yet he feared that it might be difficult to find that food; there was still no light in the world. Raven flew up through a hole in the sky, where he found another world much like our own. The daughter of the chief of heaven came by to scoop some water from a stream. Raven changed himself into a needle from a cedar tree and floated into her bucket. When the princess drank, Raven entered her body; she became pregnant, and Raven was born to her in the form of a little boy. The infant charmed the chief and his wife, who let Raven play with the box containing the light of day. Suddenly, Raven ran away with the box, resumed his original form and flew through the hole in the sky back to earth. Later, he broke the box in anger, and the sky filled up with sun, moon and stars.

The complexity, ambivalence and frequent changes of form undergone by Raven in Native American stories of the Northwest Coast can remind us of many old-world deities. Raven is a bit like the Greek Dionysus, the Norse Loki or the Hindu Siva, although he is far less anthropomorphic than any of them. For all his exuberant vitality, however, he can be a difficult figure to relate to, at least for those not initiated into the tribal cultures of his devotees. The stories can become so

The prow of a 20-metre-long canoe used by the Raven clan of the Tlingit Indians.

convoluted that the figure of Raven seems almost more a metaphysical principle than an animal. Indeed, they are, perhaps, a bit like the stories that contemporary cosmologists tell of primordial forces or particles at the beginning of the universe.

Among the Indians of the Southwest, the crow became the centre of an ecstatic ritual that, in retrospect, seems profoundly tragic. Americans usually remember the last decade of the nineteenth century as the 'Gay Nineties', a period of nearly unrestrained commercial expansion. Businessmen such as J. P.

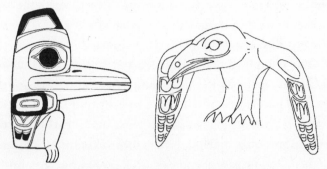

Representations of a raven carved on totem poles set up
on the northwest coast of North America.

The divinity Raven and two sea creatures copied from an 18th-century
Nootkan Indian cloak, woven of cedar bark and nettle fibre.

The Crow Dance performed by Native Americans in the 1890s, recorded by a contemporary artist.

Morgan were building enormous financial empires. Vast railway lines were being laid across North America, which opened previously forbidding areas for settlement by Europeans. Henry Ford was starting to manufacture the first American cars. But, for the American Indians, the period was anything but 'gay'. Their traditional ways of life were on the point of disappearance. The herds of buffalo, on which many had depended, were vanishing. Their reservations were being perpetually reduced in size, and the Native Americans themselves continued to fall prey to alcoholism and disease.

Around 1890, during an eclipse of the sun, a Paiute Indian named Wovoka had a vision in which he claimed to have seen God. He returned to tell his people that they must love one another, live peacefully with white people and refrain from lying or theft. God would then restore their lands to their ancestral condition. The game would return, and their ancestors would rise from the dead. The Indians would live in a rejuvenated world free from old age, disease and death. To hasten this change

Indians performed a dance for five days and nights with only brief periods of rest, during which several had visions in which they saw their forebears. Though he himself made no such claim, Wovoka was widely held by the Native Americans to be the second coming of Christ.

The new ritual brought renewed hope, but it culminated in still greater tragedy. There were soon many versions and interpretations of the Ghost Dance among different tribes.

Some believed that the rejuvenated earth would be for all Indians or for only those who accepted the prophet, while others thought that all races would share it. Some of the Sioux took the originally pacifistic doctrines of Wovoka as a counsel of war. Government authorities, meanwhile, were frightened at the union of Indians across tribal lines in rituals that seemed incomprehensible. The result was an escalation of tensions that culminated in the massacre at Wounded Knee in December of 1890 and the final destruction of traditional Native American ways of life.

The eagle had been the central bird in most mythologies of Native Americans throughout the United States, but in a time of crisis they thought more of the crow. The eagle was a symbol of the sun and the cosmic order, which might provide inspiration in normal times. In times of severe crisis, the crow, at once solar and chthonic, seemed to offer more hope of solace. The crow was more approachable, and it was also a quintessential survivor. A stuffed crow was often placed in the centre of a circle, in which the dancers moved, and the crow was also depicted on their shirts, leggings and moccasins. The dancers interpreted the cries of the crow as prophetic utterances.

In periods of desperation people have always turned to more archaic religious traditions. An example in the Bible is that during the flight from Egypt, the Hebrews reverted to the Egyptian religion and worshipped a golden calf. Later, they would almost forget Yahweh, their tribal god, but they returned to him whenever their survival as a people was threatened. Perhaps the renewed veneration of the crow, once so central to the immigrants that first crossed the Bering Strait to the New World, was similar. The Religion of the Ghost Dance was a return of a people, often considered 'primitive' in any case, to archaic, half-remembered traditions.

At the same time it was an embrace of Christianity, perhaps in a far more authentic way than that of the Europeans who had introduced the religion. The ecstatic religion of the Ghost Dance, with its millennial expectations, was more like that of the early Christians than the bureaucratized faith of European settlers. The early Christians, like the followers of the Ghost Dance, had lived in expectation of the imminent transfiguration of the world. They, also like the Indians, had based their faith more on ecstatic experience than on received doctrine. The crow in the Ghost Dance religion was roughly the equivalent of the dove, symbol of the Holy Spirit, for Jesus's original followers.

The leaders of the Ghost Dance sometimes wore the feather of an eagle, but more often they wore what was known as the wakuna. This consisted of two feathers of a crow, tied together but slightly apart from one another, which a dancer placed in his or her hair. Other dancers wore feathers as well, which were carefully painted and arranged before the ceremony. These feathers represented angelic wings, with which the dancer would ascend to heaven. One song sung during the Ghost Dance among the Arapaho went:

My children, my childen.
The wind makes the head-feathers sing –

The wind makes the head-feathers sing.
My children, my children.[1]

Still another went:

Our father, the Whirlwind,
Our father the Whirlwind,
Now wears the headdress of crow feathers,
Now wears the headdress of crow feathers.[2]

Many other songs also paid tribute to the crow.

Songs were composed and sung spontaneously during the Ghost Dance in response to visions of departed ancestors or spirits glimpsed during a trance. Yet another popular song among the Arapaho had this refrain:

The crow is circling above me,
The crow is circling above me,
The crow having come for me,
The crow having come for me.[3]

Design showing a bird, probably a crow, from a 20th-century
Hopi pottery bowl.

The dancer who composed that song saw a crow circling above his head, and believed it was an emissary to conduct him to his departed relatives.

Dances and ceremonies centring on the crow continue to be important today to Indians of the Great Plains, not so much in public ceremonies as in ritual societies. Among the Pawnee, for example, there is the Crow Lance Society. A scout, who was discovered dead by animals, founded this association. Coyotes had wished to eat his body, but crows revived him. The corvids led him to a cave, where he danced with crows for three nights. At the end of his initiation, he was given a lance covered with crow feathers, which bestowed success in hunting and war.

The Hopi Indians of the American Southwest, who traditionally live by agriculture, have often regarded the crow as a pest, though they also paid corvids a grudging respect. One Hopi story tells how a crow once invited his friend the hawk to dinner. Though the fastidious raptor would eat only freshly killed meat, the crow served him a greasy bullsnake that had already begun to decay. The hawk politely pretended to eat and even complimented the crow on his culinary art, while secretly

Crow Mother, together with the two *kachinas* with whips, who accompany her when young people are initiated in Hopi Indian society.

plotting revenge. Soon afterwards, the hawk invited the crow to dinner, and he served a putrid dish concocted from the skin and entrails of rabbits. Instead of turning away in disgust, the crow avidly devoured the meal, leaving the hawk more infuriated than ever.

The crow could also, however, be a nurturing figure. According to some Hopis, the maternal ancestor of all the *kachinas* – that is, denizens of the spirit world – was a figure known as Crow Mother. Wings of a crow sprouted from her head. She often carried a bowl for water, the source of life, and she presided over the initiation of young people into adulthood. Some Indians of the Northeastern United States, such as the New York Lenape, had myths in which a crow first brought grain to humankind.

According to one myth of the Pennsylvania Lenape, the crow once had brightly coloured feathers and a melodious voice. When the first snow began to cover up the world, they sent the crow as an emissary to the Creator. When the Creator was too busy to notice his guest, Rainbow Crow, for that was her name, captured his attention with a beautiful song. The Creator told the crow that the snow could not be stopped, but he gave the crow a torch lit from the sun. The crow carried the brand back to the earth, and warmth from the flame saved the animals. The crow, sadly, was burned until its feathers had turned black and its voice had become harsh. But for its heroism the crow has been spared from the domination of humankind, and its call still warns the animals when there is danger in the woods. Those who look carefully can still see the colours of the rainbow flash from the dark feathers of a crow.

If crows do not seem exotic to people in the industrialized world, Native Americans certainly do. This circumstance has probably encouraged the appropriation of Native American lore

Kwakiutl raven mask, photographed *c.* 1914. The Kwakiutl are known for their totem poles and elaborate costumes with which they depict myths such as those of Raven.

in the eclectic sort of spirituality known today as 'New Age'. One recent book on Native American astrology, for example, tells us that 'Raven people are extraordinary special individuals, as they act as natural catalysts for the transformation of people's lives. To achieve this, they are especially diplomatic, demonstrating great care and consideration for their fellow human beings.' It goes on to caution, however, that Raven people are prone to depression if they are denied social contact.[4] It is doubtful if this description is very faithful to Native American spirituality, and the tone is reminiscent of astrological charts on the paper tablemats of a Chinese restaurant. Many Native Americans deplore the spirituality that is marketed by others in their name.

Other Native Americans ignore, laugh at or participate in the commercialization of their heritage. At any rate, even the slickest products of popular culture contain elements of authentic spirituality. One thing that these Americans have passed on to mainstream culture, albeit in a simplistic form, is a renewed appreciation of animals such as the crow.

six
The Romantic Era

The many-wintered crow that leads
the clanging rookery home.
ALFRED, LORD TENNYSON, 'Locksley Hall'

THE MODERN WORLD has come about in such a way
that many traditional cultures have been destroyed and
many species of animals have been driven to extinction. Other creatures, like 'primitive' peoples, have become the
object of wonder and amusement in preserves and TV specials,
which celebrate what little remains of the natural world. Often
enough, a creature such as the wolf or whale has been persecuted
and romanticized at the same time. Confronting the confusions
of the present and the utter uncertainty of the future, people
have sought refuge in an idealized past, which they imagined as
more virtuous, more exciting, more civilized, more heroic or
more vital than contemporary times. In this culture of nostalgia,
the archaic image of the crow rising above a field has inspired
both fascination and fear.

What we call 'the modern world' is the result of a series of
upheavals and revolutions – social, political and technological –
over the past few centuries. People can never agree, even approximately, as to when modernity began. In a history of crows,
however, perhaps we might date it from the Great Fire of London

One of the Tower of London's ravens.

in 1666, when, at least for many urban people of England, the traditional reverence for corvids came to an abrupt end.

Ravens, as we have already seen, had long been protected in England. In September of 1666, a fire broke out in a bakery near London Bridge and burned for a week, destroying about 13,000 homes. The authorities were unable to deal with the devastation or to bury the dead, and survivors were horrified to see crows and ravens picking at charred corpses in the streets. Ravens, especially, flocked to London for the feast, where they multiplied until citizens petitioned the king to exterminate them. Vast numbers were killed and their nests destroyed. But guides today still report that Charles II remembered the legend that ravens in the Tower of London protected his kingdom; since wild ravens were no longer tolerated, he ordered that domesticated ravens be brought in, to be managed and controlled by an individual known as the Yeoman Raven Master.

It may well be that the ravens actually helped to prevent a new outbreak of bubonic plague such as the one that had claimed 75,000 lives in England during 1664 and 1665. Had the birds not eaten the dead, rats would probably have devoured the bodies, which would have been at least equally gruesome and, from the viewpoint of sanitation, far more dangerous. We can, however, hardly blame the distressed citizens of London for not thinking of this. At any rate, the fate of ravens in London was like that of the wolf and many other animals in the twentieth century – to be simultaneously sentimentalized and exterminated.

The Yeoman Raven
Master at the Tower
of London.

Feeding a Tower of London raven.

Dinner is served

The ravens and crows in the 1660s were simply behaving more or less as they always had, and people prior to the modern era had generally accepted their presence as an act of fate. By the late seventeenth century, however, that traditional stoicism was giving way. Instead of seeing them as agents of destiny, people viewed the ravens as challenging human, especially British, supremacy. The wild ravens became

LE CORBEAU ET LE RENARD. Fable I.

LE CORBEAU VOULANT IMITER L'AIGLE. Fable XXXVIII.

renegades of the civilized world. They were hunted even more vigorously in Continental Europe, in countries such as France and Germany, where traditional regard for the raven had vanished long before. In previous eras, ravens had been almost invulnerable to human weapons, but continuous improvements in firearms enabled people to virtually eliminate them from many communities. In rural America, crow shooting for sport became a popular pastime, even though people considered the meat of crows repugnant.

Nevertheless, corvids were never seriously threatened with extinction and probably even extended their range in some areas. Ravens became increasingly shy around human beings, and they sought refuge among remote cliffs and forests. Those that stayed in major urban centres made nests high in the tops of buildings, where they would be rarely seen. As for crows, they continued to live off the waste in urban areas. They reproduced so prolifically that people, with all their firearms

Battle of wits in which the crow gets the better of the fox, in an illustration from a mid-18th-century printing of fables by Jean de La Fontaine.

A raven unsuccessfully attempts to imitate an eagle, an illustration of a fable by La Fontaine.

A raven acts as a sentinel for other animals and helps to rescue them from traps, in another illustration of a fable by La Fontaine.

and poisons, soon gave up any serious aspiration to eliminate them.

A certain regard, sometimes bordering on reverence, for ravens has continued in the English countryside till this day. At the end of the eighteenth century, the pastor and naturalist Gilbert White wrote movingly of corvids in *The Natural History of Selborne*. Families of ravens had nested high above a bulge in an enormous oak on the edge of town for as long as anybody could remember. Several generations of boys had tried in vain to climb the tree, but they had given up in awe of the task. Finally, the oak was cut to provide wood for London Bridge. An opening was cut in the trunk and wedges were placed inside. Then the wood shook with the heavy blows of mallets until the trunk finally began to fall. The mother raven, however, refused to leave her nest and young, so she was thrown to the ground and killed. Pastor White, who was an exceptionally close observer and never inclined to melodrama, remarked only that 'her parental affection deserved a better fate'.[1] Readers may well see her as a martyr to industry and commerce.

As people became increasingly remote from nature, the fascination for animals actually increased. Urban legends about animals proliferated in the eighteenth and nineteenth centuries, from fantastic tales of turkeys that spoke perfect Arabic to dogs that solved murders. The story of Marie Antoinette's crow, which was at least somewhat plausible, began as the Queen of France was taking her breakfast in October of 1785 on an island in the royal estate at Versailles. She had just dipped her biscuit in a cup of milk when a crow flew down, looked at her, and began gently to beat his wings. Though initially startled, the queen gave the crow the rest of her biscuit, and a friendship between the two began. The queen would feed the bird every morning, and the crow

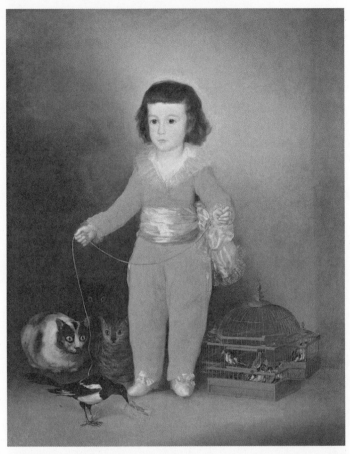

The instincts of this messenger crow, the cats and the caged songbirds are all precariously constrained within human society in Francisco Goya's *Don Manuel Osorio Manrique de Zuñiga, c.* 1786–8. But the cats may manage to eat the birds, or the crow return to the wild.

would follow her from tree to tree as she strolled about her estate. When Marie Antoinette was beheaded in 1793, the crow seemed to vanish for several years. In 1810, however, Marie Louise of Austria, who had recently married Napoleon, was breakfasting on the same island when she noticed the crow. The bird was hovering over her pavilion and cawing loudly, apparently in hope of sharing her food. When Marie Louise told Napoleon of the crow, he thought it was an omen of ill fortune and commanded her to depart from Versailles immediately. Misfortune did indeed follow, though more for the Emperor than for his consort. In 1816, after Napoleon had suffered his disastrous defeat at Waterloo and been exiled to St Helena, Marie Louise revisited the island at Versailles with her father. She suddenly heard a call, looked up, recognized the crow and cried out in terror. The gardener and servants, however, thought of the crow as an old companion. They fed the bird for the rest of its life, and visitors came from far away to see the friend of Marie Antoinette.

What could make us a little sceptical about this story is not the behaviour of the bird but that of the human beings. Unless you are a crow yourself, individual crows are hard to identify,

The crows profit from man's labour in Caspar David Friedrich's elemental scene beyond the city, *Hill and Ploughed Field near Dresden*, 1824–5.

especially from a distance. How could everybody be so sure that it was a single crow that approached Marie Antoinette, Marie Louise, and others? Couldn't it have been two or even several different birds? Whatever the case, the story illustrates how superstitions return in times of crisis. The call of a crow, once considered a bird of omen, could frighten even such a pragmatist as Napoleon.

Many writers of the nineteenth century, including serious naturalists, described animals in anthropomorphic terms that were at least as extreme as those of medieval bestiaries. One amateur naturalist in the early nineteenth century wrote that

> Rooks are proverbial for their polity, and those must give crows credit for the same talent who have witnessed the proceedings of a crow-court. These, in some respects, seem to resemble the sittings of the secret tribunal asthey are represented to have been ordered in Germany, being usually held in wild, unfrequented places, and on foggy Sundays.[2]

That era, perhaps like our own, did not really need to search the past for vivid mythologies, when such vividly imaginative stories were current. But the Romantic poets of the time felt awed, intimidated and threatened by the development of science. They mistakenly feared that rationalism might extinguish the power of human fantasy.

A good example of Romanticism is the fairy tales of Jacob and Wilhelm Grimm, published in seven editions from 1812 to 1856, which has become the most popular book of all time after the Bible in Germany and perhaps the Western world. These tales were collected by the brothers, particularly Jacob,

No crow is mentioned in the Grimm Brothers' fairy-tale of 'Hänsel and Gretel', but the early 20th-century illustrator Fritz Philipp Schmidt added this bird to serve as the witch's dark familiar.

from oral traditions, and rewritten, particularly by Wilhelm, for both commercial and artistic reasons. They are a blend of science and art, of archaic motifs and popular sentimentality, innocence and exploitation. They also appeal intensely to the imagination of nearly everybody from toddlers to the most sophisticated scholars.

The Grimm brothers' story of 'Faithful Johannes' is both one of the most archaic tales and one of the most Victorian. It opens with a young boy emerging from the sheltered world of childhood, a world that did not even exist before the early modern era. The dying king had instructed Johannes, his faithful servant, to take care of his son. The king told Johannes to show the prince everything in the castle except for one room, which contained a picture of 'the Princess of the Golden Roof'. Of course, the young king insisted on entering the room, saw the picture of the princess and fell in love with her. Then Johannes and the king kidnapped the princess in an exploit that probably goes back in oral traditions to a Viking raid, though the account was filled with flowery speeches of how the kidnapping was done out of love. The princess was delighted with the young man and plans were made for a wedding.

The next phase of the tale is especially mysterious. Faithful Johannes was sitting in the bow of the ship playing music, and three ravens approached. The birds began to talk to one another, and only Johannes – like a shaman – could understand what they said. The ravens prophesied that the princess and the young king were in danger, though the pair could still be saved. Whoever saved them, however, could not explain his actions to the king or he would be turned into stone.

This illustration by Walter Crane for 'Faithful John' in an 1886 English edition of the Grimm brothers' fairy tales reflects the eclectic blend of archaic magic, stark realism and period sentimentality of the original.

FAITHFUL·IOHN

IT HAPPENED, AS THEY WERE STILL JOURNEYING ON THE OPEN SEA, THAT FAITHFUL IOHN, AS HE SAT IN THE FORE PART OF THE SHIP, & MADE MUSIC, CAUGHT SIGHT OF THREE RAVENS FLYING OVERHEAD. THEN HE STOPPED PLAYING & LISTENED TO WHAT THEY SAID TO ONE ANOTHER

When the ship reached land, a horse came trotting up to the king. Johannes knew from listening to the ravens that the horse was about to carry his majesty off into the air, after which the king would never be seen again. As the ravens had directed, Johannes jumped on the horse, took a gun from the saddle holster and shot the horse dead. This incident resembled a horse sacrifice, a rite that has been practised not only by tribal peoples of the Arctic Circle but by Indo-Europeans from Britain to India. This was a ritual in which the spirit of a horse would be released to accompany a shaman on his journey to the other world. The ravens resemble the Celtic goddess Badbh, in her tripartite form, and other deities of the far north. The remainder of the story may sometimes read like a Victorian sermon on loyalty, but it is also filled with apparent references to archaic initiation rituals and human sacrifice.

The Grimm brothers considered their collection of German legends more important than the fairy tales, since only the legends had been literally believed. Among the most famous was the

Surrounded by family and friends, a crow is on his deathbed high up among the spewing gargoyles of Strasbourg Cathedral, in a satiric illustration of 1866 by J. J. Grandville.

Like ravens in the wild, this young medical student in a satiric illustration by J. J. Grandville of 1866 appears rather shy and aloof.

tale that the Emperor Frederick Barbarosa and his knights had not died but were sleeping in Mount Kyffhausen until God summons them. When Frederick finally awakes, he shall hang his shield on a dead tree, which will then blossom and begin a more blessed age. One day a shepherd approached the mountain, and the emperor, whose beard circled the table where he had sat in sleep, woke and asked: 'Are the ravens still flying around the mountain?' On hearing that the ravens were still there, Frederick went back to sleep for another one hundred years.[3] The circling of ravens in this tale represented time, as well as the cycle of life and death, which would draw to a close at the end of the world.

Tales from less industrialized countries were perhaps even more primeval. In the Russian fairy tales collected by Alexandr Afanas'ev in the mid-nineteenth century, corvids were filled with powerful magic. In one tale, an old farmer says 'If the Sun would warm me, if the Moon would give me light, and the Raven would help me gather the groats, I would marry my eldest daughter to the Sun, my second daughter to the Moon,

From all their pecking at dead bodies, one might indeed expect
ravens to know a lot about anatomy, as this lithograph of 1829
by J. J. Grandville suggests.

and my youngest daughter to the Raven.' His requests are
granted, and the man was true to his word. The farmer later
visited his three daughters, living with their husbands, but on
his visit to the raven he fell from the sky and died.[4] In a story
so full of cosmic imagery, it does not seem far-fetched to com-
pare the raven picking up groats to darkness devouring the
stars. In another story from Afanas'ev's collection, 'The White
Duck', magpies revive dead children by fetching the water of
speech and the water of life.

In many tales of the modern era, crows and ravens were
reminders of the archaic inheritance that is often nearly obliter-
ated but never entirely forgotten. In *Barnaby Rudge* (1841), a
historical novel by Charles Dickens set in the 1780s, the main
character, after which the novel was named, was always accompanied by a pet raven named Chip. Barnaby himself was
good-natured but uncomplicated to the point of foolishness, and
the raven was a perpetual reminder of the demonic forces that he
failed to see. The raven spoke words that were nearly nonsensical

yet often full of foreboding, and sometimes it even claimed to be the Devil.

In 1845, four years after *Barnaby Rudge* had appeared, Edgar Allan Poe first published 'The Raven'. Today, it is usually one of the first serious poems that American children read in school, and it is certainly the one that most of them remember best. Few people, however, stop to even consider what the poem might be about. What sticks in everybody's mind is only the refrain – 'Quoth the raven, "Nevermore."'

The rhythms of the poem are so insistent and the images so melodramatic that, for most readers, the meaning seems almost irrelevant. The speaker is visited by a raven late at night:

'Perched upon a bust of Pallas just above my chamber door . . .',
illustrations by Gustave Doré to Poe's 'The Raven'.

Then this ebony bird beguiling
My sad fancy into smiling,
By the grave and stern decorum
Of the countenance it wore,
'Though thy crest be shorn and shaven,
Thou,' I said, 'art sure no craven,
Ghastly grim and ancient Raven
Wandering from the Nightly shore –
Tell me what thy lordly name is
On the Night's Plutonian shore!'
Quoth the Raven 'Nevermore'.[5]

The speaker then addresses speeches and questions, which become ever more wild, to the raven, which answers all with the same word of foreboding.

The poem itself appears nearly insane in its frenzy; the author's description of its composition in a short essay entitled 'The

Poe's poem 'The Raven' has been a perennial favourite with illustrators.
This portrait of the bird is by Edmund Dulac, 1912.

Philosophy of Composition' sounds almost pathological in its analytic detachment. Like most Romantics, Poe was not greatly interested in unadulterated emotion. His artistic ideal was passion that had been subjected to discipline and control by the intellect. He managed to link the bizarre sounds and images of the poem in a coherent, if rather contrived, narrative. A tame raven that had been taught a single word, 'nevermore', had escaped its owner. A storm forced the bird to seek refuge in the room of a student, where a light was still gleaming at midnight. The young man had been poring over an esoteric volume and brooding on the death of his beloved. When the raven flew in and perched on the bust of Pallas Athena, the student began to address questions to the bird about life and death. The raven answered only 'Nevermore,' and the student became increasingly distraught. He commanded the raven to leave, but it stayed, like his melancholy torment.

Poe described with an attention to detail worthy of a professional bank-robber how he had chosen the death of a beautiful woman as the most melancholy of subjects and had heightened the sombre mood by poetic devices, such as the refrain. He chose the word 'nevermore' for its sonorous quality, and determined

The raven contemplates Poe's grave, a magazine vignette of 1880.

Paul Gauguin's etched portrait, 1891, of Stéphane Mallarmé includes a raven, since it was Mallarmé who translated Poe's poem into French.

that the constant repetition had to be accomplished by an animal. He intended a parrot at first, but decided on a raven for its prophetic reputation.

Scholars have doubted that the process of composition was as deliberate as Poe had claimed, and James Russell Lowell wrote in his 'Fable for Critics' at the end of the nineteenth century:

There comes Poe, with his raven, like Barnaby Rudge,
Three fifths of him genius and two fifths sheer fudge,
Who talks like a book of iambs and pentameters,
In a way to make people of common sense damn metres
Who has written some things quite the best of their
    kind,

Several of Aesop's fables, especially that of the jackdaw that wanted to be a peacock, have been used for political commentary in the modern world, as indeed they may have been used by Aesop.

But the heart somehow seems all squeezed out by the
    mind . . .[6]

The raven has since become the symbol of Poe, and he is
usually drawn with the bird perched on his shoulder or at his
side. More important perhaps, the raven became, and remains
so today, a standard feature in stories of Gothic horror.

If high culture emphasized the sombre and prophetic aspects
of corvids, popular culture usually stressed their playfulness. This
brings us to the history of 'Jim Crow', a name that, especially in
the United States, is synonymous with racial separation. Not many
people realize that, long before the institution of segregation, he
was a figure in popular culture.

In this French
example of
anti-German
propaganda during
the First World
War, the ape stands
for the proverbial
jackdaw that wanted
to be a peacock.

Magpies, close relatives of crows, are emblematic of the quiet of the countryside, as here in Claude Monet's *Magpie, Snow Effect, Outskirts of Honfleur*, 1868–9.

His ancestry goes back at least to the jackdaw in a popular fable traditionally attributed to Aesop, which wore coloured feathers in an unsuccessful attempt to impersonate a peacock. The story was often retold as a warning to people that aspired to rise above their social position. In aristocratic societies, the jackdaw was taken for a commoner who imitated the ways of the nobility.

The fable was often retold in the nineteenth century, as differentiations of class, wealth and nationality in Euro-American society became more intricate. The jackdaw represented any sort of pretender that ever tried to enter a sector of society that was forbidden to him. Usually, the usurper was punished, as in the Aesopian original, but occasionally his initiative was rewarded. One example was 'The Jackdaw of Rheims', a popular poem by R. H. Barham, who wrote under the pseudonym Father John Ingoldsby. Barham was an English clergyman who eventually became a minor canon of the royal chapel at Oxford. Like so many other Protestants of his time, he found Roman Catholic ritual at once enticingly beautiful and absurd. Perhaps the jackdaw of fable represented Barham's daydream of becoming – like Ingoldsby, his alter ego – a Papist. At any rate, the poem tells of a mischievous jackdaw that, drawn by the finery and the food, used to linger about at church festivities. One day, as everyone was intent on listening to a choir of holy music, the jackdaw flew off with the ring of the Cardinal. The monks and friars searched throughout the night until at last they found the ring in the jackdaw's nest. On being discovered, the jackdaw was so ashamed that he laid aside his mocking ways and lived the remainder of his life with exemplary piety. He attended every Mass and delivered gentle rebukes to anybody who lied, swore or fell asleep during a service. Finally, at his death, the jackdaw was canonized. The poem concludes:

> When as words were too faint, his merits to paint,
> The Conclave determined to make him a Saint!
> And on newly-made Saints and Popes, as you know,
> It's the custom, at Rome, new names to bestow,
> So they canonized him by the name of Jim Crow![7]

The poem was first published in 1837 and later included in Barham's highly popular collection of sketches entitled *The Ingoldsby Legends, or Mirth and Marvels*. It contains, so far as I know, the first appearance in print of the name 'Jim Crow'. The appellation here seems to suggest a sort of corvid Everyman, a 'John Doe' with black feathers.

About a decade after the appearance of 'The Jackdaw of Rheims,' however, Jim Crow had become a standard figure in the minstrel shows that became popular in the United States. These shows consisted of skits and musical acts performed by Caucasian men in 'blackface' – that is to say, painting their faces in order to impersonate black people. These performances were, needless to say, blatantly racist, and the minstrels depicted all of the stereotypes of black people as shiftless, lazy, lewd, ignorant, alcoholic and dishonest. Some black historians, however, hesitate even today to condemn the shows unequivocally, since the contempt shown towards 'Negroes' was subtly mixed with admiration. The use of blackface gave white men the opportunity to act out secret fantasies that the puritanical codes of the day would have otherwise condemned.

Odilon Redon's *The Raven*, a charcoal drawing of 1882. The bird depicted by this French Symbolist artist seems to exist in an indeterminate realm between dream and reality.

Jim Crow personified the amoral, happy-go-lucky slave that worked in the stables and hummed to himself. He was certainly, like the jackdaw of Aesop's fable, an impersonator, though it is a little difficult to say exactly how. Was Jim Crow a white person trying to be black? Or a black person trying to be white?

In any case, decades after the American Civil War, the name came to designate the enforced separation of whites and blacks. If 'Jim' represented the relatively civilized human being (supposedly, the white man), 'Crow' was the animalistic counterpart (the black man), a bit like what Freudians would later call the 'ego' and the 'id'. The minstrel show tried to combine these principles, though in a crude, bigoted sort of way, and the segregation laws would later try to separate them. Crows had more than just a dark complexion to recommend them as emblems of African-Americans. With their playfulness and unpredictability, they could easily enough be stereotyped in rather the same manner as black people.

But if the minstrel shows mocked the perceived closeness of crows – and, by association, African-Americans – to nature, creative artists often celebrated it. Just as Poe largely created the popular image of the raven, the Dutch painter Vincent van Gogh helped shape that of the carrion crow in artistic culture. When people think of crows in a cornfield, it is very often Van Gogh's paintings that first come to mind. Perhaps especially memorable is the work conventionally entitled *Wheatfield under Threatening Skies with Crows*, one of the very last paintings he produced in the summer of 1890 before committing suicide. It shows the highly stylized horizontal diagonals of crows with their wings outstretched in flight, which contrast with the vertical stalks of wheat. The crows scatter from the field to find shelter from the coming storm.

Crows seem to be a menacing force of nature in Vincent van Gogh's final painting, *Wheatfield under Threatening Skies with Crows*, 1890.

Despite his reputation as a romantic genius, Van Gogh's wonderfully eloquent letters show that he planned his paintings very consciously and deliberately. He often mentioned fields of wheat, which were symbolic of nourishment, yet he did not mention crows. Struggling to make a precarious living, Van Gogh identified with the peasants who were trying to cultivate the grain in spite of the vagaries of the weather. Shortly before his death he wrote to his brother Theo and his sister-in-law Johanna, 'There are vast fields of wheat under troubled skies, and I did not need to go out of my way to express my sadness and loneliness.' A bit later, he wrote to his mother: 'I am quite absorbed in the immense plain with wheat fields against the hills, boundless as the sea . . .'.[8]

Van Gogh deeply loved nature, yet he also saw nature as a perpetual adversary of human beings; crows could represent both sides of this ambivalence. On the one hand, they were a continuing threat to the livelihood of the agricultural workers. At the same time, however, the crows, as well as the peasants, were seeking sustenance in the fields of grain.

Like the cut flowers that Van Gogh also loved to paint, the crows belonged at once to the realms of nature and humanity. That harmony between society and nature that is so beautiful, and so precarious, in his paintings became even more difficult to sustain in the twentieth century.

seven

Lord of the Crows

Here, said they, is the Terror of the French
The scarecrow that affrights our children so.
SHAKESPEARE, *Henry IV*, I, iv

WHATEVER THE PURPOSE of scarecrows, it can't really be to keep crows away from fields. Scarecrows are colourful and entertaining, but crows are far too smart to be scared by any bundle of straw, at least for very long. So why do people make scarecrows? Fields of crops have often been destroyed by locusts and other insects but seldom or never by crows or ravens, which usually prefer bugs to grain. Crows are attracted to fields more by insects than by plants, and perhaps the service they perform to farmers by eating pests may at least compensate for the occasional vegetable snacks they grab in the process. But, even today, many farmers probably do not realize that. To see large numbers of crows settling in a cultivated field can offend a rather primitive territorial instinct in a farmer. By casually loitering about and eating grain at will, the crows can seem to be mocking the farmer's hard work.

Game animals are traditionally regarded with at least a certain gratitude and respect for the nourishment they provide. Rural people in England used to make rooks into pies, which is why the conflict between rooks and farmers often seems almost friendly.

(In the USA, immigrants from Britain and Ireland introduced rooks in the 1860s both to devour insect pests and to remind them of their former home.) In *Precious Bane*, a novel of rural life in England during the nineteenth century, Mary Webb has recorded the custom of telling the rooks when the old owner of a farm has died. After a young heir had delivered the news:

> The rooks peered down at him over their nests, and when he'd done there was a sudden clatter of wings, and they all swept up into the blue sky with a great clary, as if they were considering what was said. In a while they came back, and settled down very serious and quiet. So we knew they meant to bide. The new master expressed his relief, adding 'I be despert fond of rooky-pie.'[1]

The meat of both the carrion crow and the American crow, by contrast, is traditionally considered almost inedible. 'To eat crow' means to perform some especially repugnant penance. Folk

August Schenk, an obscure artist, perished at the hands of the Nazis, and it is tempting to read Schenk's painting *Agony* as a premonition of his fate.

This crafty 'Common American Crow' perched on a bough of fruit is an illustration of the early 1840s by John James Audubon. It seems to be gazing around carefully before robbing the farmer's produce.

etymologies trace the expression to an alleged incident in the War of 1812 between Britain and the United States. An American hunter had strayed into British territory and shot a crow. An unarmed British soldier approached the hunter, admired his marksmanship and asked to look at his gun. When the hunter handed over his weapon, the soldier turned it on him and forced the man to take a bite of the crow. The foolish officer, however, then returned the rifle, at which the hunter forced him to eat the entire bird. A few culinary adventurers have tried the meat of American crows and found it tasty. Perhaps the disdain for that food is a result, rather than a cause, of the resentment that corvids have often inspired.

At any rate, farmers have sometimes viewed crows not simply with annoyance but with hatred. In the early nineteenth century, the naturalists Alexander Wilson and Charles Bonaparte wrote of the American crow that

> he is banded as a thief and a plunderer; a kind of black-coated vagabond, who hovers over the fields of the industrious, fattening on their labours . . . Hated as he is by the farmer, watched and persecuted by almost everyone bearer of a gun . . . had not Heaven bestowed on him intelligence and sagacity far beyond common, there is reason to believe, that the whole tribe (in these parts at least) would long ago have ceased to exist.[2]

A law of 1724 passed in Pennsylvania stated that any white person who fatally shot crows could claim a reward by bringing the bodies to the local magistrate. That official would have the beaks of the crows cut off and sent to the municipal treasurer, who paid out threepence for each kill. By about 1750 it had become common for towns throughout the Eastern United States to place bounties on the lives of crows. In Massachusetts, a dead crow could be exchanged for one shilling, a bit less than one dollar in contemporary currency. A proposal to the General Assembly of Pennsylvania in 1754 asked the state to require each pioneer to shoot a dozen crows in order to claim land on the frontier. Settlers would also blow up trees that were common roosts for corvids, sometimes killing thousands at a time.

Such intense efforts did succeed in reducing the numbers of crows in American fields, but by the mid-nineteenth century farmers began to see the consequences of their absence. Crops were more threatened by worms and insects than they had ever been by birds, and states began to reconsider their bounties on the birds. Instead of shooting crows, farmers tried instead to limit avian predations, especially at certain key times of the year.

In time, many farmers in America came to regard crows with a resigned good humour, much as their British forbears had long shown towards rooks. Scarecrows often seem to be part of a sort of game of wits that people play with crows, perhaps their cleverest adversaries among animals, rather than a relentless war of extermination. Crows don't really harm farmers so much as scare them, and so perhaps scarecrows are an attempt to repay the compliment. The best scarecrows work only for a week or two before the birds figure out that they are harmless, and many never work at all. At most a scarecrow may provide a farmer with enough time to let an optimal amount of newly sown seed settle in the ground.

One old technique is to plant extra seeds, in the expectation that some will escape the ravages of birds and other pests. One verse sung when planting seeds, that goes back at least to the time of the Pilgrim Fathers in early Massachusetts goes:

> One for the cutworm,
> One for the crow,
> One for the blackbird,
> And three to grow.[3]

In strictly pragmatic terms, planting extra seed is probably the most effective way of ensuring a good harvest.

As a matter of fact, crows and scarecrows usually have a lot in common. Both tend to be somewhat scruffy, a little mischievous, and closely associated with supernatural powers. Both often seem to have a perpetual grin. The word 'scarecrow', if one stops to think about it, sounds like it might have been the name of a corvid. Perhaps the scarecrow is actually a sort of 'Lord of the Crows'? At any rate, scarecrows are frequently depicted that way, with crows perching on their arms and heads.

Our English word 'scarecrow' first meant a person employed in scaring away crows from fields in the late Middle Ages. The scarecrows, or 'scarers', might run at the crows while shouting, rattling pans or waving sticks. Some of them used homemade instruments known as 'clappers', which consisted of two pieces of wood stitched together with twine, and which rattled loudly when shaken. A scarer would stroll through the field waving his clapper at intervals and singing

> Away, away, away, birds,
> Take a little bit of corn and come another day, birds.
> Great birds, little birds, pigeons and crows,
> I'll up with my clapper and down she goes![4]

Mimbres Indian pottery design from New Mexico. Dead crows have been strung up at the edge of the field as a warning to others not to steal grain.

After all, the game of scarer versus bird was one in which neither party really had to lose in the end.

The task of scaring birds was given to young boys, and many of them must have had far more fun than profit from the work. How many children, after all, do not enjoy running and making noise! On the other hand, sensitive children must have cringed if they were ordered to destroy nests and kill the chicks inside. There is a vivid description of this occupation at the beginning of Thomas Hardy's novel *Jude the Obscure*, first published in 1895. The young hero, after whom the book is named, had been employed by a local farmer in Wessex as a scarer, and there

> The boy stood under the rick . . . and every few seconds
> used his clacker or rattle briskly. At each clack the rooks
> left off pecking, and rose and went away on leisurely wings,
> burnished like tassets of mail, afterwards wheeling back
> and regarding him warily and descending to feed at a more

respectful distance. He sounded the clacker till his armed ached, and at length his heart grew sympathetic with the birds' thwarted desires. They seemed, like himself, to be living in a world which did not want them.[5]

Jude decided to let the birds eat in peace, for which he was beaten and then fired by the farmer.

Even today, scarers are used on farms, though, like their straw brethren, their employment probably owes as much to sport and tradition as to pragmatic effectiveness. Scarecrows certainly relieve the monotony that characterized fields of grain, even before mechanized agriculture. If they don't render fields more frightening for crows, they at least make them more attractive to human beings. What we usually think of as a 'scarecrow' today is a dummy made of old clothes stuffed with straw. These figures are reputedly most effective if the clothes have been taken from

Scarecrow in North Carolina, 1930s. In an increasingly industrialized world, scarecrows have come to symbolize a traditional, rural way of life.

somebody who had shot at birds in the area, a popular idea that, whether true or false, pays a compliment to the memories of crows. One common device is to decorate the scarecrow with streamers that move in the wind, in hope that the motion will suggest a living person. Often scarecrows wear pieces of shiny metal or glass, which are intended to catch beams of sun and dazzle birds with the light.

Another common practice is to place a dead bird or two beside the dummy as a warning to the rest, a technique used by Daniel Defoe's fictional character Robinson Crusoe. It is essentially an extension of an old technique for fighting crime and sedition. The bodies of pirates or rebels would be left on the gallows or in iron cages as a warning to anyone who would defy the forces of law and order. Only a view of crows as bandits could possibly have blinded people to the ineffectiveness of such displays in the cornfield. Creatures of the woods and fields are entirely familiar with the spectacle of death. Ravens and other crows are initially alarmed by the sight of their dead, but the lifeless bodies, in any case, could not last more than a couple of days in the wild before drying out, being eaten or simply disintegrating.

Scarecrows may well go back to very ancient times, and their use has probably always been as much a matter of magic as practicality. Aelian told that the Veneti, a tribe along the Adriatic coast, would ceremonially offer carefully prepared cakes of barley, honey and oil to the jackdaws, before they began to sow. If the jackdaws accepted the offering, the Veneti believed that they could plant with confidence. Otherwise, the Veneti believed the birds would eat up the new seed and cause a famine. Such ritualistic practices would probably have been conducted on an altar, perhaps accompanied by religious images, though these have not been recorded.

Scarecrows may be ultimately descended from wooden statues of the god Priapus, which Greeks and Romans placed in fields. Priapus was the son of Dionysius, the god of wine, and Venus, the goddess of love. Despite, this exalted parentage, he was notoriously ugly, and even birds were frightened by his image. Images of Priapus showed the god with a club in one hand, and they were painted purple to make them especially terrifying. In his other hand, the god would hold a sickle, in expectation of a plentiful harvest to come.

Another theory is that scarecrows may go back to harvest dolls. These have been traditionally made of the last sheaf of a harvest. A harvest doll has sometimes been known as the 'hag' in Scotland, the 'corn dolly' in England, 'baba' in Poland, and the 'kornwolf' in Germany. The harvest doll was often ceremonially paraded through the fields and represented the spirit of the grain. The scarecrow, rising above the grain like the steeple of a medieval church above the town, does indeed seem to be the soul of the field. Scarecrows might also be related to human sacrifices in fields performed by druids to ensure a plentiful harvest. But such theories are based at least as much our intuition about scarecrows as on any concrete evidence.

In *The Owl and the Nightingale*, an anonymous English poem from the early twelfth century, there was a reference to an effigy used as a scarecrow. The nightingale and owl were exchanging taunts in a spirited debate, and the songbird mocked his sombre adversary. The owl, if shot, would be stuffed, hoisted on a pole and placed in the field to scare other birds, particularly crows. In the allegorical thinking of the Middle Ages, this image suggested the crucifix frightening away evil spirits. The owl responded by saying that his work, even in death, was more useful than the idle singing of his adversary.

All sorts of techniques have been tried to keep crows out of the fields. This illustration from the later 19th century shows Native Americans beating on pans.

In the painting representing the month of October from the *Très Riches Heures* of the Duke of Berry, painted by the Limbourg brothers in the early fifteenth century, there is an early representation of this sort of scarecrow, a dummy holding a bow and arrow. The figure does not seem to be terribly effective, since birds are following a sower in the foreground and pecking up the seeds.

By the sixteenth century, references to scarecrows in literature had become common, and there were many in the works of Shakespeare. In his play *Measure for Measure* (ii, i), Angelo, a deputy to Duke Vincentio, argues for vigorous enforcement of the laws by saying:

We must not make a scarecrow of the law,
Setting it up to fear the birds of prey,

'The habit doesn't make the monk': the scarecrow has often been used as a symbol of folly, as in this French comic strip of the early 20th century.

And let it keep one shape, till custom make it
Their perch, and not their terror.

References to scarecrows in literature have almost always been mocking and ironic. As W. B. Yeats wrote in his poem 'Among School Children', 'Old clothes upon old sticks to scare a bird.' In works of the Renaissance from Edmund Spenser on, references to scarecrows are particularly scornful. As we approach the modern period, however, the ineffectiveness of scarecrows elicited ever more sympathy and less contempt. Gradually, scarecrows have come to be valued as a form of folk art and a nostalgic reminder of our rural past.

At night scarecrows may appear as hardly more than silhouettes against the moonlit sky, and they can be pretty effective in scaring human beings who come on them suddenly. Among the Germans who settled in Pennsylvania, a scarecrow was sometimes called 'bootzamon', and American legends said that the dummies would come to life at night. Over the years the name was altered to 'bogeyman', a figure used to frighten children into good behaviour.

Perhaps the first of many stories in which the scarecrow is a major character is Nathaniel Hawthorne's 'Feathertop', first published in 1846 as part of his collection *Mosses from an Old Manse*. A New England witch named Mother Rigby tries to make the most realistic possible scarecrow to protect her fields from crows and blackbirds. The back of the scarecrow was made of a broomstick on which she had rode about at night. His body was made of splendid if faded finery from London and Paris. His head was a carved pumpkin, and his hair was made of feathers. Deciding the scarecrow was too fine to waste away in the fields, she brought him to life by giving him her magic pipe to smoke, then she sent him off to woo a young lady in town. Feathertop, for that was the scarecrow's name, proved himself a man of great charm and wit. Nevertheless, on realizing he was really just a bundle of straw, the scarecrow threw the pipe away and died.

While Hawthorne's story is largely forgotten today, it made the scarecrow an important figure in popular culture. With native wit but little confidence, Feathertop anticipated the figure that, since the start of the twentieth century, has become the model for most subsequent scarecrows in literature and even in life. The Scarecrow in *The Wonderful Wizard of Oz* (1900) by L. Frank Baum and its sequels, a fantasy based somewhat on the Middle Ages, became one of the favourite characters in children's literature. The passage in which the heroine, Dorothy, meets the scarecrow is among the most famous in children's literature. At first the scarecrow did frighten birds away but then, an old crow looked him over, and perched on his shoulder. As the scarecrow reported the exchange, the corvid first said:

'I wonder if that farmer thought to fool me in this clumsy manner. Any crow of sense could see that you are only stuffed with straw.' Then he hopped down at my feet and ate all the corn he wanted. The other birds, seeing he was not harmed by me, came to eat the corn too, so in a short time there was a great flock of them about me.

I felt sad at this, for it showed I was not such a good Scarecrow after all; but the old crow comforted me, saying 'if you only had brains in your head you would be as good a man as any of them and a better man than some of them. Brains are the only things worth having in this world, no matter whether one is a crow or a man.'[6]

Just about everybody knows what happened after that. Following many adventures, the Wizard of Oz shows that the scarecrow had really been very intelligent all along. All the straw man needed was a certificate that would acknowledge his intellect. The story anticipated trends of popular culture in the later twentieth century, in which increased self-esteem came to be presented as the solution to a vast range of personal and social ills. The wise old crow perched on the scarecrow's shoulder, as a sort of familiar, has become an iconic image in American popular culture. It is seen on posters and almost everywhere else every Halloween, though few people realize that it ultimately comes from L. Frank Baum's children's classic.

In England, the Scarecrow of Oz is rivalled in popularity by another dummy of the fields by the name of Worzel Gummidge, created by novelist Barbara Euphan Todd in 1936, whose stories have been constantly retold in radio plays, TV shows and films. Worzel, who has a cut turnip for a head and wears a black bowler hat, is a loveable but irascible rustic. He was certainly not intimidating to smaller birds. A pair of English robins made their nest in his breast pocket, and sparrows stole straw from his body. Nevertheless, he actually did a pretty decent job of frightening rooks. This success came to him, Worzel explained, because he appeared so dishevelled, and rooks, except in their nests, were lovers of order. In his relations with birds, Worzel was perhaps a bit like an uncle who could intimidate adults but was friendly to little kids.

Like so many other handmade items associated with rural life, traditional scarecrows have lost much of their, always questionable, utility but gained a nostalgic appeal in our high-tech era. Those farmers really intent on scaring crows may erect various electronic models in their fields. Some are programmed to light up at regular intervals and emit a siren like that of a fire engine. Others contain recordings of gunshot and other threatening noises. Several technologically sophisticated scarecrows also wave their limbs or spin their heads. The efficacy of these dummies in scaring crows remains uncertain, though they are pretty effective at scaring human beings.

In any case, farmers who are at all serious about trying to keep crows away must constantly innovate, in order to stay one step ahead of the birds. Catherine Elston has recently written of one farmer in Arizona, a Hopi Indian, who brought a boom box, turned up the sound and blasted rock-'n'-roll music throughout his field. When he returned the next day, there were more crows in the field than before, hopping along merrily in time to the beat.

With little remaining pretence to utility, the scarecrow has gained status as a work of art. Several rural communities in America today have annual 'scarecrow festivals' in October. There has always been a good deal of play in the construction of scarecrows, and they reflect the cultures of the nations in which they are made. The French scarecrows are dour, probably in hope that the crows will find their features especially threatening, while the optimistic American scarecrows are forever smiling. The English and Irish use their scarecrows for political and social satire. Those of Zuni Indians of the American Southwest are colourful demons, constructed of bones, rags and animal skins. The Japanese often make scarecrows in the image of the harvest god Sohodo-no-kami. Small offerings of rice cakes are sometimes left at the foot of the image, and tradition says that the deity will often make his home for the season in a scarecrow.

In the twentieth century the range and variety of scarecrows has probably increased nearly everywhere. Now they offer an opportunity for unhindered play for the imagination. Today, they are ghosts, sorceresses, vampires, dancers, space aliens, rap stars and assorted demons.

eight
The Twentieth Century and Beyond

Fare thee well! and if forever,
Still forever fare thee well. Caw! caw! caw!
SEAN O'CASEY, 'The Green Crow'

ALL WRITING OR ART about animals is an attempt to connect with the natural world, but people conceive of nature in many contrasting ways. For Van Gogh nature was still a source of harmony, but as the nineteenth century drew to a close, people were increasingly preoccupied with the violence of life in the wild. After many decades of comparative peace and prosperity, many Europeans and North Americans felt bored and restless. Thinkers such as Friedrich Nietzsche associated creatures of the wild, especially predators, with a heroic past, with the primeval vitality of Homeric heroes. This spirit filled the work of pioneers of a genre known as the 'wild animal story' such as Rudyard Kipling in Britain and Ernest Thompson Seton in North America. They thought of animals as living on an epic scale, which contrasted to the decadence of bourgeois men and women. Seton wrote in the introduction to his book *Wild Animals I Have Known* that 'The life of a wild animal always has a tragic end.' He then went on to tell stories of several animals, many of which were romantic renegades from civilization.

The art of Ivan Bilibin (1876–1942), a folklore illustrator, reflects the harshness of life in Russia in the early 20th century, with its famines, mass executions and wars.

Among his tales of animal heroes was 'Silverspot, the Story of a Crow'. Like most of Seton's animal heroes, Silverspot the crow, named for a light patch near his beak, was a warrior of extraordinary courage and resourcefulness. He led a flock of about two hundred crows on a hill near Toronto. Rather like a military officer, he drilled the crows under his charge in manoeuvres to forage or to evade threats such as armed men. The flock prospered under his leadership until one winter night he was killed by an owl. Without their leader, the crows declined in numbers and appeared doomed to oblivion.

Despite the work of a few astute observers such as Gilbert White, the study of animal behaviour had remained largely dormant from Aristotle to Darwin. By the end of the nineteenth century, it was still far from being a fully recognized academic discipline. Seton certainly had scientific aspirations, and he emphasized that all his animal stories, except for a few minor conjectures and embellishments, were true. He was the most popular naturalist of his time, though he did not have a good reputation for accuracy among his scientific colleagues. He certainly spent plenty of time among animals, and tried to record his observations with care. In the story of Silverspot, Seton even used musical notes to record the language of crows.

Paul Gauguin's *Nevermore*, 1897, alludes to Poe's poem 'The Raven', but in a ambiguous way. Perhaps the Tahitian woman, through the raven, is receiving a message from her lover.

Edouard Manet and Mallarmé interpret Poe's narrator in 'The Raven' as an aristocrat whose mansion is in an industrial metropolis. Both bird and home have become anachronisms.

In an era when many poets and novelists doubted that traditional heroism was possible and turned to 'anti-heroes' such as J. Alfred Prufrock or Leopold Bloom, Seton filled his stories of animals with valiant champions engaged in epic struggles. He always viewed animals in terms of what is sometimes called the 'great man theory of history', a perspective that emphasizes outstanding individuals rather than, say, economic or geographic conditions. Had the tales been written about human beings, they would probably have been dismissed as pulp fiction. Since, however, they were written about animals, his inclination to sentimentality and melodrama was more acceptable. Each of Seton's animal heroes became a version of Hannibal, Robin Hood or some other exalted figure of the past. As for Silverspot, he was a sort of Wyatt Earp or Wild Bill Hickok, defending a frontier community from forces of lawlessness until his tragic end. Some crows do indeed appear more authoritative than others, though the idea of a huge corvid community being led by a single charismatic individual is hard to believe. On the other hand, crows are full of surprises, and so there is no way to be sure.

The scientific study of corvids gained popularity a few decades later through the work of the renowned Austrian ethologist Konrad Lorenz, who was as charismatic as Seton and a good deal

The bird in this French advertisement from the 1920s is probably a hooded crow, a bird intimately associated with soil and weather.

'The handle of a china-cup, the gem of the collection': an illustration by Ernest Thompson Seton to his tale *Silverspot: The Story of a Crow* (1898).

more cunning. The first half of the twentieth century was dominated by the two world wars, and both naturalists thought of animals in terms of military metaphors. Lorenz joined the Nazi Party immediately after Germany's annexation of Austria in 1938, and declared in his application that 'my entire lifetime

Portrait of Silverspot by Ernest Thompson Seton.

of scientific work – in which evolutionary, racial and social-psychological questions are of foremost importance – has been in the service of National-Socialist thought.'[1] A short time later, Lorenz also became a member of the Nazi government's Office of Race Policy. After the war, he managed to conceal his political involvement, and wrote a popular book on his life with animals entitled *King Solomon's Ring*, which soon became an international bestseller.

The book was filled with cute little vignettes and cartoons. Lorenz kept a pet raven, which he once very provocatively stared at in order to confirm to himself that ravens do not peck human eyes. His colony of captive jackdaws, however, provided Lorenz with an even greater store of material. Once a large number of jackdaws mobbed him and began pecking at one of his hands. He later realized this was because his hand held a limp, black pair of bathing trunks, which resembled a baby jackdaw. His conclusion, then, was that jackdaws have a defensive instinct that could be triggered by sight of somebody holding any object resembling a chick.

Nevertheless, the author's background as a Nazi theorist was apparent in his harsh view of nature as a forum of domination and perpetual conflict. Just as Ernest Thompson Seton had been fixated on individual greatness, so Lorenz was preoccupied with hierarchy. He claimed to have observed that the jackdaws in his

A meditative jester is joined in his solitude by a crow, a sort of 'wise fool', in this early 20th-century English book-plate.

FREDERICK

FEAR GOD

FEAR NOUGHT

LOCKER

Pablo Picasso, *Woman with a Crow*, 1904. Due perhaps to the influence of Dickens and Poe, ravens came to be thought of as the companions of outcasts and eccentrics.

London *Evening Standard* cartoon of 10 June 1940: Himmler and other Nazis are portrayed as ravens, bringing disaster in their wake.

colony were precisely organized in a pyramidal structure – every jackdaw knew precisely which animals were ranked above or below him, exactly as in an army. Some jackdaws that Lorenz had identified as high-ranking, however, would often not assert themselves in relation to their presumed inferiors. How then, could one be sure that the ranks were correctly assigned? Perhaps ranks were not transitive or in constant flux? Lorenz did not even consider these possibilities but offered another explanation: 'Very high caste jackdaws are most condescending to those of lowest degree and consider them as the very dust beneath their feet . . .'.[2] The flock of jackdaws, in other words, was like a huge corporation where the VP will not even deign to speak to the assembly-line workers. People have always described societies of animals in terms of familiar institutions, making them into monarchies, armies, socialist republics or whatever was the current fashion of the day.

Seton and Lorenz were, as already noted, near the beginning of the study of animal behaviour, which has become vastly more complex and sophisticated since the mid-twentieth century. Both naturalists ignited intense controversies about the scientific status of their methods, and the debates continue up to the present. Seton and Lorenz were unabashedly anthropomorphic. In other words, they attributed human reactions to animals. One trouble with this approach to animals is that, since society changes constantly, anthropomorphism starts to sound dated very quickly. The models used by Lorenz and Seton now often no longer seem either bestial or human. Even corporations today, for the most part, are no longer as hierarchal as Lorenz's jackdaws.

In the meantime, popular culture was even more anthropomorphic than the work of any naturalists. The identification of crows with black Africans, established in minstrel shows through the figure of Jim Crow, was to continue in less virulent forms throughout the twentieth century. In the 1941 animated film *Dumbo, the Flying Elephant*, the hero, a young elephant with enormous ears, is often accompanied by crows who speak in heavy Southern accents and come across like black workers on a plantation. They sing, in a bluesy sort of way, 'I think I'll have seen just about everything / When I see an elephant fly.' Nevertheless, the crows are clearly on the side of the hero. They offer Dumbo support and understanding, and they even help him develop his talent for flight. Also slightly controversial are the two crows Heckel and Jeckel, who starred in a series of cartoons by Warner Brothers that were very popular in the United States during the 1950s and '60s. Like Bugs Bunny and many other cartoon characters of the time, they were wisecracking tricksters, a bit like stereotypal street hustlers of the black slums. But the images of corvids that have come down to us from biblical times, whether good or evil, have rarely been lacking in dignity. The twentieth century was filled with apocalyptic disasters on the scale of the Old Testament, including concentration camps and nuclear bombs. There are now threats of even greater devastation by ecological collapse or terrorism. In the first half of the twentieth century, the Portuguese author Miguel Torga addressed these fears in his story 'Vincent the Raven', based on the biblical tale of Noah and his Ark. The raven, an animal in the Ark, became angry that the animals and the earth should be punished for the crimes of humankind. At last he left the Ark unbidden, perched on the peak of Mount Ararat, and called out his defiance to God. The flood continued to rise, but Vincent refused to leave. God finally realized that, should he drown Vincent, his creation would no longer be complete, so he relented and reluctantly allowed the waters to recede. Vincent is in the tradition of Jewish prophets and sages who, like Abraham before Sodom and Gomorrah, would question, bargain with and even defy God, in the name of justice.

It was in a similar spirit that the Irish dramatist Sean O'Casey (1884–1964) chose the crow as his symbol. 'A common bird, the crow', he wrote, 'as I am a common man, as are we all'.[3] He told a story of one tall, bushy female crow that aroused the anger of local farmers by stealing the eggs from their hen-houses. One evening O'Casey saw an English officer named Sergeant Roche, who was known as a crack shot, catch the notorious robber in a tree. The Sergeant slowly raised his gun, and the onlookers thought the crow would shortly be blown to splinters. The shot, however, never came. The crow seemed to have disappeared, though none had seen her fly away or heard the flap of wings. Suddenly, in the distance, they heard the mocking call of the bird. O'Casey did not have to explain the meaning of the incident to his countrymen. The crow would surely have reminded them of Irish rebels defying and eluding their British rulers over the centuries.

O'Casey saw himself, more specifically, as a 'green crow', that is, a raven. Green, as everybody knows, was the colour worn by the Irish rebels following the Wexford rebellion of 1798. The raven is a bird that usually appears black but may also be either green or even purple, depending on the angle at which it is struck by light. This was like the Irish nationalists who, under British rule, concealed their true loyalties from adversaries but revealed them to their friends. O'Casey had, in fact, been denounced by many nationalists, who felt he had abandoned the Irish cause for the more universal ideals of socialism. His response to these critics was, in effect, that the raven was green, even if this might not be apparent to everybody; in much the same way, O'Casey was Irish. The dramatist also felt that the struggles of the Irish, like the trials and tribulations of the ancient Hebrews, had a universal meaning. The crow was all people that survived by their wits in a world dominated by powerful institutions such as the British Empire.

But the British poet Ted Hughes saw the cleverness of crows less as peasant shrewdness than as infernal magic. In Hughes's collection of poems entitled *Crow* (1970), the protagonist was voracious and pitiless yet indestructible. One poem near the beginning, 'Examination at the Womb-door', ends:

Who is stronger than hope? *Death*
Who is stronger than the will? *Death*
Stronger than love? *Death*
Stronger than life? *Death*
But who is stronger than death?

Me, evidently.
Pass, Crow.

Crow goes on to match his wits against the elements and even against God. He tries, like modern human beings, to relieve his endless boredom with technological devices from cars to a rocket crashing on the moon. Though sometimes defeated, Crow always manages to survive.

All cultural upheavals invariably have a conservative side, since a disruption of the *status quo* allows buried traditions to surface. In the case of crows, these traditions include chthonic associations, which reach back long before Christianity and Judaism. One example is in the novel *A Fine and Private Place* by Peter Beagle. This story was based partly on that of the biblical prophet Elijah, who had retreated into the wilderness, where he was fed by ravens and eventually granted a vision of the resurrected dead. The novel is set in the graveyard of a contemporary suburban community in the USA, where an eccentric pharmacist named Mr Rebok lives in a graveyard. He speaks to, and welcomes, the spirits of the dead, and a talking raven steals sandwiches to feed him. Just as Mr Rebok is caught between the worlds of the living and the departed, the raven uneasily straddles nature and human civilization. Like many other idealists, the raven spoke of his service with a humour that could verge on being cynical: 'Ravens are pretty neurotic birds,' the corvid says. 'We're closer to people than any other bird and we're bound to them all our lives, but we don't have to like them.' Mr Rebok eventually leaves the graveyard to unite two ghosts named Michael and Laura, who have led unfulfilled and uneventful lives, in the hope that they might be reborn through love. The novel ends with the raven, no longer needed, circling in the distance, no doubt observing people with the same sardonic humour as before.

The modern world has created all sorts of unions of folk-loric and religious traditions that were formerly kept apart by barriers of doctrine and geography. These movements cover a vast range from folk religions such as voodoo and Santeria, which are based largely in the poor neighbourhoods of Latin America and the Caribbean, to New Age spirituality, which appeals mostly to the middle class of Europe and North America. In all of these syncretic movements, the crow or raven is an important icon. Marie Laveau, a powerful sorceress in the nineteenth century who was known as the 'Voo-doo Queen of New Orleans', has at times allegedly returned from the dead in the form of a crow.

It is hard to say to what extent it reflects, or carries over into, real life today, but many movies and popular entertainments appear based on a pre-Christian code of honour, in which revenge is a sacred duty. A good example is the movie *The Crow*, directed by Alex Proyas, which was released in 1993 and quickly became the centre of a cult. It concerns a young rock musician named Alex Draven, who has been murdered together with his fiancée by a gang of thugs on Halloween. Guided by a crow, Darven returns from the world of the dead to seek revenge. The crow leads him to each of the murderers, and Draven punishes them, one by one, with an agonizing death. Scenes of the crow in flight separate each episode in this cinematic saga of retribution. The movie is technically well done, but it would be rather unre-markable if not for its young star Brandon Lee, the son of kung fu legend Bruce Lee and a master of the martial arts himself, who plays Draven. Throughout the movie are scenes in which gang-sters attempt to kill Draven with bullets or knives, only to see that weapons cannot hurt a man who is already dead. In filming one of the final scenes, however, a gun intended to fire blanks had actually been loaded. Brandon was fatally wounded and died twelve hours later. After an extensive investigation, police determined that the killing of the charismatic young actor had been an accident, but rumours and legends have continued to circulate about it ever since. Was the star actually assassinated by a martial arts society for revealing secrets? Was he murdered for privately investigating the Chinese underworld? Did footage of the killing actually appear in the film? The film was followed by a series of movies on TV and graphic comic books based on the story. The ghostly smile of Draven with a crow beside him became an iconic image for fans of fantasy and horror throughout the United States and beyond.

And what of earthly crows? The study of animal behaviour has grown far more refined in latter half of the twentieth century, and several researchers have devoted much of their careers to the study of corvids. Lawrence Kilham, for example, has carefully watched groups of crows and meticulously recorded his observations. Bernd Heinrich, whose orientation is more empirical, has conducted numerous field experiments in which he has tried to understand the social structures of ravens by leaving out carcasses and noting how news of these baits seems to spread among the birds.

For all the refinements in their methodology, however, what such researchers have come up with is often a lot of 'sometimes' and quite a bit of 'perhaps'. As a graduate student who had taken a fancy to ravens, Heinrich had been told by his mentor, 'Ravens . . . are smarter than you are, and it will take you years to outwit them enough to so that you can begin to get meaningful data.'[4] After devoting much of a lifetime to the study of ravens, Heinrich wrote:

Having now lived on intimate terms with ravens for many years, I have seen amazing behavior that I had not read about in the more than 1,400 research reports and articles on ravens in the scientific literature, and that I could never have dreamed were possible. I have become skeptical that the interpretation of all ravens' behavior can be shoehorned into the same programmed and learned responses–categories as those of bees. Something else is involved . . . Ultimately, knowing all that goes on in their brains is, like infinity, an unreachable destination.[5]

He found that ravens, like human beings, were highly individual and prone to behave in unpredictable ways.

Corvids, and their societies, are flexible to a point where it is very difficult to generalize from the behaviour of a few. Like

Design from a proto-Viking picture stone of the 5th or 6th century AD. Two warriors do battle while a bird, possibly a crow, waits to devour the body of the vanquished.

Fabric design by the Woodland Indians of the American Northeast,
a large linguistic and cultural group that includes the Lenape.

human beings, they have cultures; they may be capable of adapting to a wide range of circumstances, including, for example, being watched by scientists. Why do corvids collect in large numbers in certain groups of trees during autumn and winter? Well, why do people collect in places like Central Park? You may put the latter question to scores of social scientists, psychologists and novelists, and all will come up with very different answers. They will variously emphasize things like power, social contact, food, spirituality, sex, nature, money, fear and so on, depending on their own interests and priorities. Most of the answers will sound fairly plausible, but none will be really complete. Every answer will tell something about the crowds but a lot more about the speaker.

Much the same thing may be said of those who write about the crows that assemble on rooftops or in trees. A certain degree of anthropomorphism is inevitable in addressing such a question, and this will reflect the psychology of the researcher. If a scientist says crows do it for protection, that might, for example, be because she feels insecure. If a scientist says they do it to socialize, the answer may reflect his own loneliness. Corvid behaviour may have so many facets that it will never be entirely explained.

In the later twentieth century and after, crows have been among the very few elements of an urban landscape that appear truly wild. With their sleek, black colour, crows are usually conspicuous, especially when seen against the snow or a bright morning sky. They are also loud, and their cries, if not exactly musical, are certainly exuberant. It is very odd that people do not take more notice of crows, but that does not necessarily mean that crows are not important to us.

We often ignore crows in large part simply because we do not have much pragmatic reason for paying attention to them. We know ways to exploit most animals that live in close proximity to human beings. Pigeons, for example, are eaten and used to carry messages. Rats and rabbits are used in experiments by the millions every year. Crows are among the very few creatures that manage to occupy approximately the same habitats as human beings while doing us, in pragmatic ways at least, very little good or harm. They often give an impression of sublime indifference to people, as though waiting patiently for the era of human beings to pass. Their major use to people, when there has been one, was generally as a divine sign or portent.

Perhaps the fact that we take crows for granted most of the time actually shows a special sort of intimacy. In much the same way, we fail to notice the faces passing by us on a busy street.

Kiki Smith's *Three Crows* sculpture, 1995, may have been modelled crucifixion-style after actual birds that dropped from the sky, killed by toxic fumes or pesticides.

When, however, people do start to notice crows, it is often in times of crisis, as even staidly rational men and women begin to look around for guidance from fate. The crow evokes a feeling of wonder that is never dissipated through familiarity. And in this, as in so many other ways, crows are a lot like human beings.

Timeline of the Crow

The family Corvidae probably originates in the land mass that is present-day Australia

30–20 million BC

The continents are drifting closer together, and Corvidae cross into Asia, followed by rapid evolutionary differentiation, as the birds spread to Europe and America

***c.* 12,000 BC**

In the Last Ice Age the carrion crow and hooded crow begin to diverge

***c.* 10,000 BC**

Shamanic cult of the raven begins to spread from Siberia and Central Asia throughout much of the northern hemisphere

***c.* 3,000 BC**

According to legend, Noah sends out a raven from the Ark, but land is not found; later he sends the dove and the Ark comes to rest on Mount Ararat

***c.* AD 20**

A talking raven, hatched on the roof of the temple dedicated to Castor and Pollux, flies to the forum every day and salutes the Emperor Tiberius and others by name. The bird is murdered, outraged citizens kill the perpetrator and a magnificent funeral for the bird is attended by a vast crowd (Pliny)

***c.* AD 225**

St Paul the Hermit takes refuge in a forest cave in order to escape the Emperor Decius. Every day a crow brings him half a loaf of bread. On one occasion St Paul is visited by St Anthony, and the crow brings an entire loaf (Jacob de Voragine, *The Golden Legend*, *c.* 1290)

***c.* AD 500**

In a British battle between the armies of Arthur and Owein, the latter's forces are magical ravens, able to recover from wounds and even rise from the dead, and they come close to defeating Arthur's men ('The Dream of Rhonabwy' in the *Mabinogion*)

***c.* AD 620**

According to legend, Muhammad hides in a cave to escape his enemies. A crow, then a white bird, tries to betray the prophet and is punished by Muhammad by being turned black and cursed forever

1785

Marie Antoinette adopts a pet crow at Versailles, which she feeds every morning

1812

First edition published of the Grimm brothers' *Fairy Tales*, which include stories with corvids in them

1845

Edgar Allen Poe publishes his poem 'The Raven'

1862–74

Corvids are introduced into New Zealand to help control insects

1890

Van Gogh paints *Wheatfield under Threatening Skies with Crows*, one of his very last paintings

c. 600 BC	c. 500 BC	c. 330 BC	c. 200 BC	c. 43 BC
According to Apollodorus, the maiden Coronis made love to Apollo but marries a young man named Ischys. The crow, which was then white, brings news of the marriage to Apollo, who turns the crow black out of anger	Ravens are buried in pits by Celts during the Iron Age; one at Winklebury was deliberately arranged with wings outstretched at the bottom of a hole, probably a ritual sacrifice	In *Historia Animalium*, Aristotle says that both 'raven' (*corax*) and 'crow' (*corone*) are birds that prefer to live in towns	A Celtic helmet of iron buried in Ciumesti, Romania, is topped by an image of a raven with hinged wings that would flap as the wearer enters battle	The city of Lyon, *Lugdunum*, meaning 'Raven's Hill', is founded, the settlers having followed the flight of ravens to the site

AD 864	1349	1555	1667	1754
A Viking discovers Iceland by releasing a raven and sailing after it (*Saga of Flokki*)	Konrad von Megenberg, in his popular natural history, reports that ravens will deliberately peck out the eyes of mules or oxen on a farm	Pierre Belon reports that it is forbidden in England under penalty of a heavy fine to do any harm to ravens, which are needed to consume carrion and so prevent disease (*L'Histoire de la Nature des Oyseaux*)	Charles II orders domesticated ravens for the Tower of London, under the Yeoman Raven Master	A proposal to the General Assembly of Pennsylvania asks the state to require each pioneer to shoot a dozen crows in order to claim land on the frontier

1900	1930s	1970	1993	2002
L. Frank Baum publishes *The Wonderful Wizard of Oz*, which includes the Scarecrow	Austrian ethologist Konrad Lorenz has a pet raven and a colony of captive jackdaws providing him with a store of material for his theories	Ted Hughes publishes his collection of poems entitled *Crow*	*The Crow*, a film directed by Alex Proyas, quickly becomes the centre of a cult	In Alex Kacelnik's Oxford lab, a crow figures out how to bend a wire to make a hook with which to retrieve food. Chimps and monkeys fail to duplicate the feat

REFERENCES

INTRODUCTION

1 David Quamen, 'Has Success Spoiled the Crow?', *Natural Acts: A Sidelong View of Science and Nature* (New York, 1985), pp. 30–31.
2 Keith Thomas, *Man and the Natural World* (New York, 1983), p. 138.
3 Burton Stevenson, ed., *The Macmillan Book of Proverbs, Maxims, and Famous Phrases* (New York, 1948), p. 1501.

2 EGYPT, GREECE AND ROME

1 John Pollard, *Birds in Greek Life and Myth* (New York, 1977), p. 179.
2 *Babrius and Phaedrus*, trans. Ben Edwin Perry (Cambridge, MA, 1965), p. 446.
3 Aesop, *The Complete Fables*, ed. and trans. Olivia and Robert Temple (New York, 1998), p. 37.
4 'The Comedy of Asses', in *Plautus*, trans. Paul Nixon (Cambridge, MA, 1961), vol. I, lines 259–61.
5 Pliny, *Natural History*, trans. H. Rackham, W.H.S. Jones et al. (Cambridge, MA, 1953), vol. 10, book X, chap. LX, part 121.
6 *Suetonius*, trans. J. C. Rolfe (Cambridge, MA, 1997), book XXIII, section 2.
7 In *Catullus/Tibullus/Pervigilium Veneris*, ed. G. P. Goold, trans. J. P. Postgate (Cambridge, MA, 1962), book II, song VI, lines 19–20.

3 THE EUROPEAN MIDDLE AGES AND RENAISSANCE

1 Caroline Larrington, trans., *The Poetic Edda* (New York, 1996), p. 54.
2 Hugh of Fouilloy, *The Medieval Book of Birds: Hugh of Fouilloy's Aviarium*, trans. Willene B. Clark (Binghamton, NY, 1992), pp. 174–5.
3 Seamus Heaney, trans., *Beowulf* (New York, 2000), lines 2440–44.
4 Arthur Quiller-Couch, ed., *The Oxford Book of Ballads* (Oxford, 1910), p. 67.

5 Richard Muir, *The English Village* (New York, 1980), p. 127.
6 Al-Qazwini, Hamdullah Al-Mustaufa, *The Zoological Section of the Nuzhatu-L-Qulāb*, ed. and trans. J. Stephenson (London, 1928), pp. 21, 81.
7 Edward Topsell, *The Fowles of Heaven, or History of Birdes*, ed. Thomas P. Harrison and F. David Hoeniger (Austin, TX, 1972), p. 229.

5 NATIVE AMERICAN CULTURE

1 James Mooney, *The Ghost Dance Religion and the Sioux Outbreak of 1890* (Chicago, 1965), p. 214.
2 Ibid., p. 219.
3 Ibid., p. 234.
4 Debbie Burns, *Animal Totem Astrology: How to Use Native American Totems to Uncover your Unique Relationship to Nature and the Seasons* (Sydney, 2001), p. 35.

6 THE ROMANTIC ERA

1 Gilbert White, *The Natural History of Selborne* (New York, c. 1890), p. 9.
2 William Stewart Rose, *Apology Addressed to the Traveler's Club, or Anecdotes of Monkeys* (London, 1825), p. 168.
3 Jacob and Wilhelm Grimm, *The Complete Fairy Tales of the Brothers Grimm*, trans. Jack Zipes (New York, 1987), vol. 1, legend 23.
4 Alexandr Afanas'ev, *Russian Fairy Tales*, trans. Norbert Guterman (New York, 1973), pp. 588–9.
5 'The Raven', in *Last Flowers: The Romance Poems of Edgar Allan Poe and Sarah Whitman* (Providence, RI, 1987), p. 5.
6 James Russell Lowell, *A Fable for Critics, by James Russell Lowell; with vignette portraits of authors de guibus fabula narratur* (London, 1890), p. 78.
7 R. H. Barham (Thomas Ingoldsby, pseud.), *The Ingoldsby Legends, or Mirth and Marvels* (London, 1866), p. 132.
8 Bruce Bernard, ed., *Vincent by Himself: A Selection of Van Gogh's Paintings and Drawings Together with Extracts from his Letters* [letters trans. Johanna Van Gogh] (Boston, MA, 1985), p. 214.

7 LORD OF THE CROWS

1 Mary Webb, *Precious Bane* (New York, *c.* 1960), p. 45.
2 Alexander Wilson and Charles Lucian Bonaparte, *American Ornithology, or The Natural History of Birds in the United States*, 4 vols, ed. Robert Jameson (Edinburgh, 1831), I, pp. 237–8.
3 James Giblin and Dale Ferguson, *The Scarecrow Book* (New York, 1980), p. 28.
4 Ibid., p. 18.
5 Thomas Hardy, *Jude the Obscure* (New York, 1961), p. 19.
6 L. Frank Baum, *The Wonderful Wizard of Oz* (New York, 1960), p. 47.

8 THE TWENTIETH CENTURY AND BEYOND

1 Benedikt Föger and Klaus Taschwer, *Die Andere Seite des Spiegels: Konrad Lorenz und der Nationalsozialismus* (Vienna, 2001), p. 79.
2 Ibid., p. 147.
3 Sean O'Casey, *The Green Crow* (New York, 1956), p. vii.
4 Bernd Heinrich, *Ravens in Winter* (New York, 1989), p. 59.
5 Bernd Heinrich, *Mind of the Raven* (New York, 1999), p. xxi.

BIBLIOGRAPHY

Aelian, *On Animals*, 3 vols, trans. A. F. Scholfield (Cambridge, MA, 1971)

Aesop, *The Complete Fables*, ed. and trans. Olivia and Robert Temple (New York, 1998)

Afanas'ev, Alexandr, *Russian Fairy Tales*, trans. Norbert Guterman (New York, 1973)

Al-Qazwini, Hamdullah Al-Mustaufa, *The Zoological Section of the Nuzhatu-L-Qulāb*, ed. and trans. J. Stephenson (London, 1928)

Angell, Tony, *Ravens, Crows, Magpies, and Jays* (Seattle, WA, 1978)

Apollonius of Rhodes, *The Voyage of Argo*, trans. E. V. Rieu (New York, 1971)

Aristophanes, 'The Birds', in *Aristophanes*, 3 vols, trans. Benjamin Bickley Rogers (Cambridge, MA, 1974), Ii, pp. 123–30

Aristotle, *Historia Animalium*, vol. I (books I–X), ed. D. M. Balme (Cambridge, 2002)

Associated Press, 'Smart Crow Makes Her Own Tools to Get Food – Research', *Daily Hampshire Gazette* (8 August 2002), p. C10

Babrius and Phaedrus, trans. Ben Edwin Perry (Cambridge, MA, 1965)

Barham, R. H. (Thomas Ingoldsby, pseud.), *The Ingoldsby Legends, or Mirth and Marvels* (London, 1866)

Baum, L. Frank, *The Wonderful Wizard of Oz* (New York, 1960)

Beagle, Peter S., *A Fine and Private Place* (New York, 1992)

Belon du Mans, Pierre, *L'Histoire de la Nature des Oyseaux: Facsimilé de l'édition de 1555* (Geneva, 1997)

Bernard, Bruce, ed., *Vincent by Himself: A Selection of Van Gogh's Paintings and Drawings Together with Extracts from his Letters* [letters trans. Johanna Van Gogh] (Boston, MA, 1985)

Bierhorst, John, *Mythology of the Lenape* (Tucson, AZ, 1995)

Buck, William, trans., *Ramayana* (Berkeley, CA, 1976)

Burns, Debbie, *Animal Totem Astrology: How to Use Native American Totems to Uncover your Unique Relationship to Nature and the Seasons* (Sydney, 2001)

Campbell, Joseph, *Historical Atlas of World Mythology*, 4 vols (New York, 1988)

Cervantes, Miguel de, *Adventures of Don Quixote*, trans. J. M. Cohen (New York, 1988)

Christie, Anthony, *Chinese Mythology* (New York, 1996)

Cicero, *The Nature of the Gods and On Divination*, trans. C. D. Yonge (Amherst, MA, 1997)

Cleansby, Richard, and Gudbrand Vigfusson, *An Icelandic–English Dictionary* (Oxford, 1957)

Coombs, Franklin, *The Crows: A Study of Corvids in Europe* (London, 1978)

Dähnhardt, Oskar, *Naturgeschichtliche Volksmärchen*, 2 vols, 3rd edn (Leipzig, 1909)

Davis, Courtney, and Dennis O'Neil, *Celtic Beasts: Animal Motifs and Zoomorphic Design in Celtic Art* (London, 1999)

Dickens, Charles, *Barnaby Rudge* (New York, 1966)

Disney Studios, *Dumbo*, video, 60th anniversary edition (Los Angeles, 2001)

Dolan, Edward F., *Animal Folklore: From Black Cats to White Horses* (New York, 1992)

Elston, Catherine Feher, *Ravensong: A Natural and Fabulous History of Ravens and Crows* (Flagstaff, AZ, 1991)

Ferguson, Gary, *The World's Great Nature Myths* (Helena, MT, 1996)

Föger, Benedikt, and Klaus Taschwer, *Die Andere Seite des Spiegels: Konrad Lorenz und der Nationalsozialismus* (Vienna, 2001)

Fontenay, Elizabeth de, *Le silence des bêtes: La philosophie à l'épreuve de l'animalité* (Paris, 1998)

Giblin, James, and Dale Ferguson, *The Scarecrow Book* (New York, 1980)

Giles, Herbert A., trans., *Strange Stories from a Chinese Studio* (New York, 1926)

Gill, Sam D., and Irene F. Sullivan, *Dictionary of Native American Mythology* (New York, 1992)

Goodchild, Peter, *Raven Tales: Traditional Stories of Native Peoples* (Chicago, 1991)

Goodwin, Derek, *Crows of the World* (Ithaca, NY, 1976)

Grantz, Jeffrey, trans., *Early Irish Myths and Sagas* (New York, 1981)

——, trans., *The Mabinogion* (New York, 1976)

Green, Miranda, *Celtic Myths* (Austin, TX, 1993)

——, *Animals in Celtic Life and Myth* (New York, 1992)

Grimm, Jacob, and Wilhelm, *The Complete Fairy Tales of the Brothers Grimm*, trans. Jack Zipes (New York, 1987)

——, *The German Legends of the Brothers Grimm*, 2 vols, ed. and trans. Donald Ward (Philadelphia, 1981)

Gubernatis, Angelo de, *Zoological Mythology or Mythology of Animals* (Chicago, 1968)

Haining, Peter, *The Scarecrow: Fact and Fable* (London, 1988)

Hardy, Thomas, *Jude the Obscure* (New York, 1961)

Hawthorne, Nathaniel, *The Old Manse* (Bedford, MA, 1997)

Heaney, Seamus, trans., *Beowulf* (New York, 2000)

Heinrich, Bernd, *Ravens in Winter* (New York, 1989)

Herodotus, *Herodotus*, 4 vols, trans. A. D. Godley (New York, 1926)

Hitakonanu'larxk, *The Grandfathers Speak: Native American Folk Tales of the Lenape People* (New York, 1994)

Hole, Christina, E. Radford and M. A. Radford, *The Encyclopedia of Superstitions* (New York, 1996)

Homer, *The Iliad*, trans. A. T. Murray (Cambridge, MA, 1967)

Houlihan, Patrick F., *The Animal World of the Pharaohs* (New York, 1996)

Hugh of Fouilloy, *The Medieval Book of Birds: Hugh of Fouilloy's Aviarium*, trans. Willene B. Clark (Binghamton, NY, 1992)

The Jerusalem Bible, Reader's Edition, ed. Alexander Jones (Garden City, NY, 1968)

Joyce, P. W., ed., *Old Celtic Romances: Tales from Irish Mythology* (New York, 1962)

Kilham, Lawrence, *The American Crow and the Common Raven* (College Station, TX, 1989)

Kors, Alan C., and Edward Peters, eds, *Witchcraft in Europe 1100–1700: A Documentary History* (Philadelphia, 1972)

Larrington, Caroline, trans., *The Poetic Edda* (New York, 1996)

Leeming, David, and Margaret Leeming, *A Dictionary of Creation Myths* (New York, 1994)

Livy, *Livy*, 14 vols, trans. B. O. Foster (Cambridge, MA, 1960)

Lorenz, Konrad Z., *King Solomon's Ring: New Light on Animal Ways*, trans. Marjorie Kerr Wilson (New York, 1952)

Lowell, James Russell, *A Fable for Critics, by James Russell Lowell; with vignette portraits of authors de guibus fabula narratur* (London, 1890)

Maolotki, Ekkehart, ed., *Hopi Animal Stories* (Lincoln, NE, 2001)

Martin, Bobi, *All About Scarecrows* (Fairfield, CA, 1990)

Megenberg, Konrad von (Conrad von Alemann), *Das Buch der Natur* [reprint of the original edn of 1348–9] (Stuttgart, 1861)

Mooney, James, *The Ghost Dance Religion and the Sioux Outbreak of 1890* (Chicago, 1965)

Muir, Richard, *The English Village* (New York, 1980)

Neal, Avon, and Ann Parker, *Scarecrows* (Barre, MA, 1978)

Nelson, R. K., *Make Prayers to the Raven: A Koryukan View of the Northern Forest* (Chicago, 1983)

Nicol, C. W., *The Raven's Tale* (Madeira Park, BC, 1993)

O'Casey, Sean, *The Green Crow* (New York, 1956)

Ovid, *Fasti*, trans. James G. Frazer (Cambridge, MA, 1996)

—, *Metamorphoses*, trans. Rolfe Humphries (Bloomington, IN, 1955)

Pausanias, *Description of Greece*, 5 vols, trans. W.H.S. Jones (Cambridge, MA, 1959–61)

Plautus, 'The Comedy of Asses', *Plautus*, trans. Paul Nixon (Cambridge, MA, 1961), vol. I, pp. 123–230

Pliny, *Natural History*, 10 vols, trans. H. Rackham, W.H.S. Jones et al. (Cambridge, MA, 1953)

Plutarch, *Greek Lives: A Selection of Nine Greek Lives*, trans. Robin A. Waterford (New York, 1999)

—, 'On the Use of Reason by Irrational Animals,' *Essays*, trans. Robin Waterfield (New York, 1992), pp. 38–9

Poe, Edgar Allan, 'The Philosophy of Composition', *Readings on Edgar Allan Poe*, ed. Bonnie Szumski (San Diego, CA, 1998), pp. 137–47

—, 'The Raven', *Last Flowers: The Romance Poems of Edgar Allan Poe and Sarah Whitman* (Providence, RI, 1987), pp. 11–13

Poignant, Roslyn, *Oceanic Mythology* (New York, 1967)

Pollard, John, *Birds in Greek Life and Myth* (New York, 1977)

Proyas, Alex (Director), *The Crow*, video-cassette (Burbank, CA: Buena Vista Home Video, 1994)

P'u Sung-ling, *Strange Stories from a Chinese Studio*, trans. Herbert A. Giles (New York, 1926)

Quamen, David, 'Has Success Spoiled the Crow?', in *Natural Acts: A Sidelong View of Science and Nature* (New York, 1985), pp. 30–35

Quigley, Christine, *The Corpse: A History* (London, 1996)

Quiller-Couch, Arthur, ed., *The Oxford Book of Ballads* (Oxford, 1910)
Reid, Bill, and Robert Bringhurst, *The Raven Steals the Light* (Seattle, WA, 1988)

Ritter, Johann, and Carl Kesslar, eds, *Geseze der Republik Pennsylvanien* (Reading, PA, 1807)

Roob, Alexander, *Alchemy and Mysticism* (New York, 1997)

Rose, William Stewart, *Apology Addressed to the Traveler's Club, or Anecdotes of Monkeys* (London, 1825)

Rowland, Beryl, *Birds with Human Souls: A Guide to Bird Symbolism* (Knoxville, TN, 1978)

Sax, Boria, *Animals in the Third Reich: Pets, Scapegoats, and the Holocaust* (New York, 1999)

—, *The Parliament of Animals: Anecdotes and Legends, 1750–1900* (New York, 1992)

Saxe, John Geoffrey, 'The Blind Men and the Elephant' [after a passage in the *Udana*, a Hindu scripture], *Elephants Ancient and Modern*, ed. F. C. Sillar and R. M. Meyer (New York, 1968), pp. 139–40

Schochet, Elijah, *Animal Life in Jewish Tradition: Attitudes and Relationships* (New York, 1984)

Scott, Sir Walter, *Letters on Demonology and Witchcraft* (1832)

Seidelman, Harold, and James Turner, *The Inuit Imagination: Arctic Myth and Sculpture* (New York, 1994)

Seton, Ernest Thompson (*pseud.* of Ernest Seton Thompson), *Wild Animals I Have Known* (New York, 1900)

Shakespeare, William, *The Complete Works*, ed. David Bevington, 4th edn (Boston, 1997)

Stevenson, Burton, ed., *The Macmillan Book of Proverbs, Maxims, and Famous Phrases* (New York, 1948)

Stone, Brian, trans., *The Owl and the Nightingale/ Cleanness/ St Erkenwald*, 2nd edn (New York, 1988)

Suetonius, *Suetonius*, trans. J. C. Rolfe (Cambridge, MA, 1997)

Thomas, Keith, *Man and the Natural World* (New York, 1983)

Thompson, D'Arcy Wentworth, *A Glossary of Greek Birds* (London, 1936)

Tibullus, *Catullus/Tibullus/Pervigilium Veneris*, ed. G. P. Goold, trans. J. P. Postgate (Cambridge, MA, 1962), pp. 192–339

Todd, Barbara Euphan, *Worzel Gummidge, or The Scarecrow of Scatterbrook* (New York, 1941)

Toperoff, Sholomo Pesach, *The Animal Kingdom in Jewish Thought* (Northvale, NJ, 1995)

Topsell, Edward, *The Fowles of Heaven, or History of Birdes*, ed. Thomas P. Harrison and F. David Hoeniger (Austin, TX, 1972)

Torga, Miguel, 'Vincente the Raven', *Farrusco the Blackbird and Other Stories from the Portuguese*, trans. Denis Brass (London, 1950), pp. 83–8

Tymoczko, Maria, *Two Death Tales from the Ulster Cycle: The Death of Cu Roi and The Death of Cu Chulainn* (Dublin, 1981)

Van Laan, Nancy, *Rainbrow Crow: A Lenape Tale* (New York, 1991)

Virgil, *The Singing Farmer: A Translation of Virgil's 'Georgics'*, trans. L.A.S. Jermyn (Oxford, 1947)

Voragine, Jacobus de, *The Golden Legend: Readings on the Saints*, 2 vols, trans. William Granger Ryan (Princeton, NJ, 1995)

Waddell, Helen, *Beasts and Saints* (Grand Rapids, MI, 1996)
Webb, Mary, *Precious Bane* (New York, c. 1960)
White, Gilbert, *The Natural History of Selborne* (New York, c. 1890)
Wilson, Alexander, and Charles Lucian Bonaparte, *American Ornithology, or The Natural History of Birds in the United States*, 4 vols, ed. Robert Jameson (Edinburgh, 1831)
Yeats, W. B., *The Poems of W. B. Yeats* (New York, 1983)

ASSOCIATIONS AND WEBSITES

CITY OF RAVENS
www.facebook.com/Tower.Ravens
A Facebook page by the author of this book, giving links and news relating
to crows and ravens in human culture.

CORVID CORNER
http://corvidcorner.com
A delightfully idiosyncratic website where people throughout the world
exchange pictures, lore, videos, news and experiences relating to corvids.

CROWS: THE LANGUAGE AND CULTURE OF CROWS
www.crows.net
A site devoted to research into the culture and communication
of the American crow.

DEBBY PORTER
www.debbyporter.com/corvidae
The website of Debby Porter, with links to many other sites relating
to all aspects of crows and ravens.

KEVIN J. MCGOWAN
http://birds.cornell.edu/crows
The site of Kevin J. McGowan, an ornithologist at Cornell University,
who specializes in crows. Enquiries concerning corvid behaviour ecology
will result in a gracious and informed response.

LIVING WITH WILDLIFE
http://wdfw.wa.gov/living/crows.html
A website run by the American state of Washington, containing
very practical information and advice for people who wish to
observe or interact with corvids in the wild.

PET CROWS AND RAVENS WEBRING
www.angelfire.com/nj2/corax/ring.html
A site where people exchange tips, experiences and information
about keeping crows and ravens as pets.

ACKNOWLEDGEMENTS

I would like to thank my wife, Linda Sax, for many suggestions and for encouragement in the course of writing this book. Many thanks go also to Marion W. Copeland, who assisted me with her enormous knowledge of animals in modern literature. Bob Reiser called my attention to the story of Rainbow Crow and other important tales. I am also grateful to Jonathan Burt, a scholar as well as the editor of the Animal series, who first suggested that I write this book.

Since starting to write about crows, I have become far more aware of their presence in my everyday routines, and they have provided me with thought, instruction and entertainment. If the reader experiences something similar, this book will have fulfilled its major purpose.

PHOTO ACKNOWLEDGEMENTS

The author and publishers wish to express their thanks to the below sources of illustrative material and/or permission to reproduce it. While every effort has been made to identify and credit copyright holders, we would like to apologize to anyone who has not been formally acknowledged.

Bibliothèque Nationale de France: pp. 42, 87; from Sebastian Brant, *Doctor Brants Narrenschiff* (Basel, 1499): p. 72; British Library, London: pp. 61, 63; Cleveland Museum of Art, Ohio: p. 83; Courtauld Institute Galleries, London: p. 150 (top); from E. H. Eaton, *Birds of New York*, 2 vols (Albany, NY, 1910/14): p. 26; from Jesse Walter Fewkes, *Hopi Katcinas Drawn by Native Artists* (Washington [DC], 1904): p. 101; from [Jean de la Fontaine], *Fables Choisies, mises en vers par J. de la Fontaine*, 4 vols (Paris, 1755–9): pp. 108 (foot), 109; from Arthur Charles Fox-Davies, *A Complete Guide to Heraldry* (Edinburgh, 1909): pp. 12, 20, 49, 74; from J. W. von Goethe, *Reineke Fuchs* (Stuttgart, 1857): p. 66; from J. J. Grandville, *Les Animaux* (Paris, 1866): pp. 30, 32, 116, 117, 118; Hamburger Kunsthalle: p. 112

(photo Elke Walford/Hamburger Kunsthalle/bpk Berlin); from *Harper's Weekly*, XXV/1285 (6 August 1881): p. 124; from *Household Stories from the Brothers Grimm* (New York, 1866): p. 115; from William Jardine, ed., *The Naturalist's Library*, vol. II: *Ornithology. Birds of Great Britain and Ireland*, Part II (Edinburgh, 1853): p. 34; from Austen Henry Layard, *Nineveh and Its Remains*, vol. II (New York, 1849): p. 35; photos Library of Congress, Washington, DC (Prints and Photographs Division): pp. 8 (photo Edward Curtis), 103, 139 (photo John Vachon); Metropolitan Museum of Art, New York (Jules Bache Collection): p. 111 (photo © 1994 MMA); from the Rev. F. O. Morris, *A History of British Birds*, vol. II (London, 1855): pp. 13, 16, 28, 78; Musée d'Orsay, Paris: p. 126 (photo RMN/Hervé Lewandowski, © ADAGP); Museo del Prado, Madrid: pp. 70, 75; National Gallery of Canada, Ottawa: p. 128; New College Oxford: p. 69; photo National Anthropological Archives, Suitland, Maryland: p. 97; National Gallery of Victoria, Melbourne: p. 133; National Palace Museum, Taipei, Taiwan: p. 91; from Edgar Allan Poe, *The Bells and Other Poems* (New York and London, 1912): pp. 121; from Edgar [Allan] Poe, *Le Corbeau* [:] *The Raven* [:] *Poéme par Edgar Poé* (Paris, 1871): p. 150 (foot); from Edgar Allan Poe, *The Raven* (New York, 1884): pp. 119, 120; from Jean-Baptiste Samat, *Les Chiens, Le Gibier et ses Ennemis* (Saint-Etienne, 1907): p. 10; from Ernest Thompson Seton, *Wild Animals I Have Known* (London, 1899): p. 152; from Edmund J. Sullivan, *The Kaiser's Garland* (London, 1915): p. 125; Toledo Museum of Art, Toledo (photo TMAH/Succession Picasso, DACS 2003), p. 154; Trinity College, Dublin: pp. 57, 59; Van Gogh Museum, Amsterdam (Vincent Van Gogh Foundation): p. 130; photo Ellen Page Wilson, courtesy of Pace Wildenstein, New York: p. 165.

INDEX